The New York Times

IN THE HEADLINES

The Gender Pay Gap

EQUAL WORK, UNEQUAL PAY

THE NEW YORK TIMES EDITORIAL STAFF

Published in 2019 by The New York Times® Educational Publishing in association with The Rosen Publishing Group, Inc.
29 East 21st Street, New York, NY 10010

First Edition

The New York Times
Alex Ward: Editorial Director, Book Development
Phyllis Collazo: Photo Rights/Permissions Editor
Heidi Giovine: Administrative Manager

Rosen Publishing
Megan Kellerman: Managing Editor
Julia Bosson: Editor
Greg Tucker: Creative Director
Brian Garvey: Art Director

Cataloging-in-Publication Data
Names: New York Times Company.
Title: The gender pay gap: equal work, unequal pay / edited by the New York Times editorial staff.
Description: New York : New York Times Educational Publishing, 2019. | Series: In the headlines | Includes glossary and index.
Identifiers: ISBN 9781642821185 (library bound) | ISBN 9781642821178 (pbk.) | ISBN 9781642821192 (ebook)
Subjects: LCSH: Pay equity—United States—Juvenile literature. | Equal pay for equal work—United States—Juvenile literature. | Discrimination in employment—Juvenile literature. | Discrimination in employment—United States—Juvenile literature.
Classification: LCC HD6061.2.U6 G463 2019 | DDC 331.2'1530973—dc23

Manufactured in the United States of America

On the cover: Despite legislation for equal pay, the gender pay gap persists; Spark Studio/Imagezoo/Getty Images.

Contents

CHAPTER 3

The Economics of the Pay Gap

CHAPTER 4

Solving the Pay Gap

CHAPTER 5

The Pay Gap Abroad

Introduction

EACH APRIL, activists across the country celebrate an unusual holiday: Equal Pay Day, the date selected by the National Committee on Pay Equity that represents how much longer women have to work in order to equal what men earned the previous year. This disparity is known as the gender pay gap: In other words, when factoring in education level, work experience and seniority, women still earn less money than men do in the same position.

The gender pay gap has been an intractable fact of American life for as long as women have been a part of the workforce. In 1963, President John F. Kennedy signed the Equal Pay Act, an addendum to the Fair Labor Standards Act that had created minimum wage and overtime pay requirements. At the time, women made 59 cents for every dollar paid to their male counterparts. More than 50 years later, the wage gap has lessened but still persists: By the mid-1990s, women earned about 75 cents to a man's dollar. That number had not changed much by 2018, when experts put the amount closer to 80 cents to a man's dollar, although the figure changes when factors such as race, education level and gender identity are taken into account. This pay disparity exists across nearly every industry, from the red carpets of Hollywood to the hallways of hospitals, resulting in a significant lifetime disparity in wealth between the genders.

But what causes the gender pay gap? And how can it be resolved? These questions are not always so clear cut. Experts can agree that one major cause for the gender pay gap comes from the consequences of motherhood on a woman's career. Without a maternity leave package in place that protects a woman's position, a woman will be forced to decide between her job and a family. Many experts also

Lilly Ledbetter, whose struggle for pay equal to that of her male co-workers inspired the Fair Pay Act of 2009, introduces President Barack Obama at the White House in Washington on April 8, 2014.

emphasize the importance of paid paternity leave to ease the burden on mothers.

But the roots of the wage gap are more complicated than just parenthood. Social theorists suggest it might be a consequence of ingrained sexism in society. Men are more likely to negotiate higher salaries and to ask for raises, while many women fear that asking for more money will make them seem less likable.

In Washington, action to counteract the wage gap has been mixed. In 2007, the Supreme Court ruled on a case brought by Lilly Ledbetter, a former employee of the Goodyear Tire and Rubber factory who learned that she was paid less than her sixteen male colleagues, including those with less seniority. In a 5-4 decision, the Supreme Court found that she had waited too long to bring the complaint to court, reducing the ability of plaintiffs to sue for wage discrimination. Barack Obama made equal pay a signature issue of his

2008 campaign, and in January of 2009, the Lilly Ledbetter Act was the first bill he signed as president.

Wage discrimination lawsuits remain famously difficult to prosecute. As a result, companies, activists and legislators have developed creative solutions. In some industries, executives have made salary information public and allowed employees to discuss wages openly. In Massachusetts in 2016, Governor Charlie Baker signed a bill making it illegal for employers to ask an applicant's salary in a job interview, requiring them to state a compensation up front based on the employee's potential worth to the company. The goal behind this legislation is to ensure that the historically low wages often assigned to women and minorities don't follow them for their entire careers.

Ultimately, the wage gap is not just an American issue. A gender-based disparity exists across many Western nations, from Iceland to Britain to Australia. But as many of the experts in this book attest, the first step to combatting this issue is understanding its impact. The New York Times continues to highlight the struggle to bridge the wage gap. With these articles, we can envision a world in which equal work will bring equal pay.

CHAPTER 1

The Pay Gap Over the Decades

By the early 1980s, women earned about 65 cents for every dollar men earned, only about a six-cent improvement since the Equal Pay Act went into effect on June 10, 1964. The gap shrank to about 75 cents over the next 15 years, but employers found ways to continue to underpay women, partly because women tended to work in lower-paid industries. The articles in this chapter demonstrate how progress on pay equity was halting and inconsistent in the decades after the Equal Pay Act was passed.

Law in Effect Today Bans Job Discrimination Based on Sex

BY DAMON STETSON | JUNE 10, 1964

A NEW LAW prohibiting wage discrimination throughout the nation on the basis of sex will go into effect tomorrow.

Although the law was designed primarily to protect women from discriminatory pay practices, it gives the same protection to men.

The measure, known as the Equal Pay Act of 1963, amends the Fair Labor Standards Act and applies nationally to about 27.5 million employees, including 7.4 million women.

A recent survey by Prentice-Hall, publishers of a personnel management service, indicated that most companies already had or would adjust sex-based differentials by increasing women's rates or by transferring male employees to other jobs. In the future, the survey showed, many companies may segregate male and female job classifications.

The new law was passed by Congress a year ago and signed by President Kennedy. To allow time, however, for adjustment to the equal-pay provisions, full compliance was not required for a year.

In addition, the act provides for a further deferment for employes covered by collective bargaining agreements until their terminations, if not later than June 11, 1965.

Major provisions of the Equal Pay Act include:

• Employers are required to pay equal wages within their establishments to men and women doing equal work on jobs requiring equal skill, effort and responsibility.

• Employers may not reduce the wage rate of any employee to eliminate a prohibited wage differential based on sex.

• A union representing employees may not cause or attempt to cause an employer to discriminate against an employee in violation of the equal-pay provision.

On the other hand, the law does not prohibit payment of wages at lower rates to one sex where the differential is based on a seniority system, a merit system, a system measuring earnings by quantity or quality of production, or any other factor other than sex.

The act will be administered and enforced by the Wage and Hour and Public Contracts Divisions of the United States Department of Labor. Wages withheld in violation of the equal-pay provisions, according to the department, will have the status of unpaid minimum wages or unpaid overtime compensation.

The Wage and Hour Division may supervise payment of back wages or, in certain cases, the Secretary of Labor may bring suit for back pay upon the written request of the employee involved.

Surveys by the Labor Department prior to passage of the new law last year showed that some industries had a double standard of pay under which men receive more money than women for the same job.

These studies showed that women, in some cases, received $8 to $20 a week less than men for the same type of office work.

The pay offered to female college graduates was found to be substantially lower than that offered to male graduates.

The study by Prentice-Hall of the effect of the law on employers suggested that in some cases the Equal Pay Act might limit job opportunities for women.

Some employers, it said, are overwhelmed by the prospect of analyzing and re-evaluating jobs and wages and would segregate existing job classifications wherever possible.

On the other hand, the survey indicated the long range effect of the law might result in greater opportunity for promotion of qualified women employees. Many employers, it reported, said they were willing to consider women for higher-rated jobs on the same basis as men.

Court Cases Reveal New Inequalities in Women's Pay

BY ROBERT PEAR | AUG. 21, 1985

CONGRESS OUTLAWED the most blatant forms of employment discrimination against women more than 20 years ago, but Federal judges and other Government officials report that employers have found new, more subtle ways to justify paying women less than men. Courts have accepted some of the justifications and rejected others, depending on the facts of each case.

Ruth Weyand, a lawyer at the Equal Employment Opportunity Commission, the Federal agency responsible for enforcing many anti-discrimination laws, said that "employers often refuse to describe or recognize what a woman does, and they are happy to pay her less, well knowing what she does."

Miss Weyand noted, for example, that a woman may be called a secretary and paid a secretary's wages, though she does the buying for a company, as would a purchasing officer or a contracting officer.

The debate over subtler forms of discrimination is only remotely related to the dispute over the doctrine of "comparable worth," which holds that men and women should be paid the same for different jobs having the same intrinsic value.

Last week, the Administration took a first step in implementing President Reagan's opposition to the comparable worth principle by siding with the State of Illinois in a case brought by the Illinois Nurses Association and the American Nurses Association.

Responding today to the Government's action, Eunice Cole, president of the American Nurses Association, said: "It culminates many months of ridicule of the principle of pay equity for working women by this Administration."

Quite apart from that kind of dispute, the Equal Pay Act of 1963 established the principle of equal pay for equal work, regardless of sex.

The law provides that no employer shall discriminate on the basis of sex by paying wages to employees within the same establishment "at a rate less than the rate at which he pays wages to employees of the opposite sex" for "equal work." Jobs are said to be equal if they require "equal skill, effort and responsibility" and are performed under similar working conditions.

This law, in the words of the United States Court of Appeals for the Third Circuit, in Philadelphia, was "intended as a broad charter of women's rights in the economic field." But the law allowed exceptions to the principle of equal pay for equal work when one sex is paid less because of a seniority system, a merit system or a system that measures earnings by the quantity or quality of production.

There is another general exception where the differential is based on any factor other than sex. A company might pay higher wages, for example, to a man who was reassigned to a lower-paying job because of a physical disability or a reduction in the company's work force.

Employers have repeatedly asserted that their pay differentials fit into one of the four exceptions, and they offer a range of justifications for paying men more than women. They contend, for example, that men perform extra duties justifying higher pay.

In white-collar industries such as banking, they sometimes argue that the men are in a special training program or have superior academic credentials. Or they say that merchandise sold by men is more profitable than goods sold by women, so the employer is justified in paying them higher commissions. This argument has been made, for example, by clothing stores.

Likewise, employers argue that they have to pay men more than women to lure them into taking a particular job. Or they set wages on the basis of prior salary, so that for the same job the women end up with lower pay than the men, who have historically received higher compensation.

Winn Newman, a lawyer who has represented labor unions in pay equity cases, said that until the mid-1960's "there were all sorts of overt, blatant restrictions on women that legalized discrimination."

State laws supposedly designed to protect women said, for example, that they could not work more than five hours without a rest period, could not work after midnight and could not hold jobs requiring them to lift more than 15 pounds. Most such protective laws have been repealed by state legislatures or nullified by courts.

Edward E. Potter, a labor lawyer who represents employers in pay discrimination cases, said the "pay gap" would tend to disappear "when you have more upward mobility programs, more training and education programs to facilitate the entry of women into traditionally male jobs."

The Supreme Court has held that employers violate the law by paying men and women unequal wages for jobs that are very much alike but not "identical in every respect." In finding that Corning Glass Works had violated the equal pay law, the Court said that inspectors on the day and night shifts had done "substantially equal" work. The men, who were night inspectors, did a certain amount of packing, lifting and cleaning not done by the women who were their counterparts on the day shift. But the extra work, the Court said, was "of little consequence."

Where the extra duties are incidental or secondary tasks, courts have rejected the employer's argument that they justify higher pay for men. This has happened in cases involving women who are hospital aides and men who are orderlies. The primary work of both is to care for patients, and the women often perform some of the same additional duties as the men.

A number of cases have involved maids and janitors. Employers contend that they are justified in paying higher wages to janitors, most of them men, because they expend more effort in operating machinery, making repairs, moving furniture or shoveling snow. But, as with hospital aides and orderlies, some maids performed the same duties and did other chores as well, such as making beds and cleaning sinks, toilets or mattresses.

In one case, the First Citizens Bank of Billings, Mont., explained that female tellers had been paid less than a man performing the same work because he was enrolled in a management training program. The United States Court of Appeals for the Ninth Circuit ruled this year that "no formal program or manual existed." The bank estimates that it would have to pay $75,000 in back pay. It is appealing the decision to the Supreme Court.

Similarly, an Iowa bank said it was justified in paying higher wages to men because they were in a training program. But a Federal district judge rejected this explanation, saying the program did not provide formal instruction and had not included women.

Courts have also held that a college degree does not necessarily justify higher pay, especially where the college education is not necessary or relevant to the job. "While not discounting the value of a college education," Federal District Judge E. Gordon West said in 1977 in a Louisiana case, "we do not believe it justifies the wage differential" between men and women managing pizza shops.

But the United States Court of Appeals for the Third Circuit, in Pennsylvania, has held that Robert Hall Clothes Inc. was justified in paying a higher salary to the men who sold men's clothing than to the women who sold women's clothing.

Judge James Hunter 3d said, "The merchandise in the men's department was, on the average, of higher price and better quality than the merchandise in the women's department," and the men's department was more profitable. The wage differential, he said, was thus legal under the Equal Pay Act because it was based on a "factor other than sex."

To avoid embarrassment to customers, only men worked in the men's clothing department and only women worked in the women's department. The propriety of such segregated employment was not an issue in the case.

By contrast, another Federal appeals court held that a chain of health spas in Detroit was not justified in paying lower commissions to managers who were women than to those who were men.

The men were paid 7.5 percent of the amount generated from sales of memberships, while the women were paid 5 percent. Since the health spas sold more memberships to women than to men, the total remuneration for the employees, both men and women, was about the same.

The United States Court of Appeals for the Sixth Circuit struck down this arrangement, noting that the Equal Pay Act "commands an equal rate of pay for equal work." In this case, it said, "women had to produce more to be paid the same as men," and they were selling exactly the same product.

Courts have repeatedly held that "market forces" alone do not justify lower pay for women doing the same, or substantially the same, work as men. In the Corning Glass case, the pay disparity arose because men would not work for the low wages paid to women inspectors. The company's decision to take advantage of that situation was "understandable as a matter of economics," the Supreme Court said, but it became illegal after passage of the Equal Pay Act.

The market operates on the basis of competition, but in the equal pay law, Congress declared that a wage differential based on sex "constitutes an unfair method of competition."

The United States Court of Appeals for the Ninth Circuit, in California, ruled that an insurance company could use prior salary as a factor in setting wages for newly hired sales agents if the company could demonstrate legitimate business reasons for such a formula.

The women, supported by the Equal Employment Opportunity Commission, had argued that the formula would perpetuate historic patterns of sex discrimination. The Allstate Insurance Company said that starting salaries were based on numerous factors including experience, ability and education, as well as prior salary. In settling the lawsuit, the company last year agreed to pay $5 million to about 3,100 women who had worked as sales agents or trainees, but it denied having discriminated against them.

By most accounts, then, women have made substantial progress, but have not achieved full pay equity. "The Equal Pay Act, as interpreted by the courts, reaches a small minority of working women," Miss Weyand, the lawyer at the Equal Employment Opportunity Commission, said. "Most women still work in jobs that are overwhelmingly sex-segregated."

Gender Pay Gap, Once Narrowing, Is Stuck in Place

BY DAVID LEONHARDT | DEC. 24, 2006

THROUGHOUT THE 1980S and early '90s, women of all economic levels — poor, middle class and rich — were steadily gaining ground on their male counterparts in the work force. By the mid-'90s, women earned more than 75 cents for every dollar in hourly pay that men did, up from 65 cents just 15 years earlier.

Largely without notice, however, one big group of women has stopped making progress: those with a four-year college degree. The gap between their pay and the pay of male college graduates has actually widened slightly since the mid-'90s.

For women without a college education, the pay gap with men has narrowed only slightly over the same span.

These trends suggest that all the recent high-profile achievements — the first female secretary of state, the first female lead anchor of a nightly newscast, the first female president of Princeton, and, next month, the first female speaker of the House — do not reflect what is happening to most women, researchers say.

A decade ago, it was possible to imagine that men and women with similar qualifications might one day soon be making nearly identical salaries. Today, that is far harder to envision.

"Nothing happened to the pay gap from the mid-1950s to the late '70s," said Francine D. Blau, an economist at Cornell and a leading researcher of gender and pay. "Then the '80s stood out as a period of sharp increases in women's pay. And it's much less impressive after that."

Last year, college-educated women between 36 and 45 years old, for example, earned 74.7 cents in hourly pay for every dollar that men in the same group did, according to Labor Department data analyzed by the Economic Policy Institute. A decade earlier, the women earned 75.7 cents.

The reasons for the stagnation are complicated and appear to include both discrimination and women's own choices. The number of women staying home with young children has risen recently, according to the Labor Department; the increase has been sharpest among highly educated mothers, who might otherwise be earning high salaries. The pace at which women are flowing into highly paid fields also appears to have slowed.

Like so much about gender and the workplace, there are at least two ways to view these trends. One is that women, faced with most of the burden for taking care of families, are forced to choose jobs that pay less — or, in the case of stay-at-home mothers, nothing at all.

If the government offered day-care programs similar to those in other countries or men spent more time caring for family members, women would have greater opportunity to pursue whatever job they wanted, according to this view.

The other view is that women consider money a top priority less often than men do. Many may relish the chance to care for children or parents and prefer jobs, like those in the nonprofit sector, that offer more opportunity to influence other people's lives.

Both views, economists note, could have some truth to them.

"Is equality of income what we really want?" asked Claudia Goldin, an economist at Harvard who has written about the revolution in women's work over the last generation. "Do we want everyone to have an equal chance to work 80 hours in their prime reproductive years? Yes, but we don't expect them to take that chance equally often."

Whatever role their own preferences may play in the pay gap, many women say they continue to battle subtle forms of lingering prejudice. Indeed, the pay gap between men and women who have similar qualifications and work in the same occupation — which economists say is one of the purest measures of gender equality — has barely budged since 1990.

Today, the discrimination often comes from bosses who believe they treat everyone equally, women say, but it can still create a glass ceiling that keeps them from reaching the best jobs at a company.

"I don't think anyone would ever say I couldn't do the job as well as a man," said Christine Kwapnoski, a 42-year-old bakery manager at a Sam's Club in Northern California who will make $63,000 this year, including overtime. Still, Ms. Kwapnoski said she was paid significantly less than men in similar jobs, and she has joined a class-action lawsuit against Wal-Mart Stores, which owns Sam's Club.

The lawsuit is part of a spurt of cases in recent years contending gender discrimination at large companies, including Boeing, Costco, Merrill Lynch and Morgan Stanley. Last month, the Supreme Court heard arguments in a case against Goodyear Tire and Rubber.

At Sam's Club, Ms. Kwapnoski said that when she was a dock supervisor, she discovered that a man she supervised was making as much as she was. She was later promoted with no raise, even though men who received such a promotion did get more money, she said.

"Basically, I was told it was none of my business, that there was nothing I could do about it," she said.

Ms. Kwapnoski does not have a bachelor's degree, but her allegations are typical of the recent trends in another way: the pay gap is now largest among workers earning relatively good salaries.

At Wal-Mart, the percentage of women dwindles at each successive management level. They hold almost 75 percent of department-head positions, according to the company. But only about 20 percent of store managers, who can make significantly more than $100,000, are women.

This is true even though women receive better evaluations than men on average and have longer job tenure, said Brad Seligman, the lead plaintiffs' lawyer in the lawsuit.

Theodore J. Boutrous Jr., a lawyer for Wal-Mart, said the company did not discriminate. "It's really a leap of logic to assume that the data is a product of discrimination," Mr. Boutrous said. "People have different interests, different priorities, different career paths" — and different levels of desire to go into management, he added.

The other companies that have been sued also say they do not discriminate.

Economists say that the recent pay trends have been overlooked because the overall pay gap, as measured by the government, continues to narrow. The average hourly pay of all female workers rose to 80.1 percent of men's pay last year, from 77.3 percent in 2000.

But that is largely because women continue to close the qualifications gap. More women than men now graduate from college, and the number of women with decades of work experience is still growing rapidly. Within many demographic groups, though, women are no longer gaining ground.

Ms. Blau and her husband, Lawrence M. Kahn, another Cornell economist, have done some of the most detailed studies of gender and pay, comparing men and women who have the same occupation, education, experience, race and labor-union status. At the end of the late 1970s, women earned about 82 percent as much each hour as men with a similar profile. A decade later, the number had shot up to 91 percent, offering reason to wonder if women would reach parity.

But by the late '90s, the number remained at 91 percent. Ms. Blau and Mr. Kahn have not yet examined the current decade in detail, but she said other data suggested that there had been little movement.

During the 1990s boom, college-educated men received larger raises than women on average. Women have done slightly better than the men in the last few years, but not enough to make up for the late '90s, the Economic Policy Institute analysis found.

There is no proof that discrimination is the cause of the remaining pay gap, Ms. Blau said. It is possible that the average man, brought up to view himself the main breadwinner, is more committed to his job than the average woman.

But researchers note that government efforts to reduce sex discrimination have ebbed over the period that the pay gap has stagnated. In the 1960s and '70s, laws like Title VII and Title IX prohibited discrimination at work and in school and may have helped close the pay gap in subsequent years. There have been no similar pushes in the last couple of decades.

Women have continued to pour into high-paid professions like law, medicine and corporate management where they were once rare, but the increases seem to have slowed, noted Reeve Vanneman, a sociologist at the University of Maryland.

Medicine offers a particularly good window on these changes. Roughly 40 percent of medical school graduates are women today. Yet many of the highest paid specialties, the ones in which salaries often exceed $400,000, remain dominated by men and will be for decades to come, based on the pipeline of residents.

Only 28 percent of radiology residents in 2004-5 were women, the Association of American Medical Colleges has reported. Only 10 percent of orthopedic surgery residents were female. The specialties in which more than half of new doctors are women, like dermatology, family medicine and pediatrics, tend to pay less.

Melanie Kingsley, a 28-year-old resident at the Indiana University School of Medicine, said she had wanted to be a doctor for as long as she could recall. For a party celebrating her graduation from medical school, her mother printed up invitations with a photo of Dr. Kingsley wearing a stethoscope — when she was a toddler.

As the first doctor in her family, though, she did not have a clear idea of which specialty she would choose until she spent a summer working alongside a female dermatologist in Chicago. There, she saw that dermatologists worked with everyone from newborns to the elderly and worked on nearly every part of the body, and she was hooked.

"You get paid enough to support your family and enjoy life," said Dr. Kingsley, a lifelong Indiana resident. "Yeah, maybe I won't make a lot of money. But I'll be happy with my day-to-day job, and that's the reason I went into medicine — to help other people." She added: "I have seen people do it for the money, and they're not very happy."

The gender differences among medical specialties point to another aspect of the current pay gap. In earlier decades, the size of the gap was similar among middle-class and affluent workers. At times, it was actually smaller at the top.

But the gap is now widest among highly paid workers. A woman making more than 95 percent of all other women earned the equivalent of $36 an hour last year, or about $90,000 a year for working 50 hours a week. A man making more than 95 percent of all other men, putting in the same hours, would have earned $115,000 — a difference of 28 percent.

At the very top of the income ladder, the gap is probably even larger. The official statistics do not capture the nation's highest earners, and in many fields where pay has soared — Wall Street, hedge funds, technology — the top jobs are overwhelmingly held by men.

Justices' Ruling Limits Suits on Pay Disparity

BY LINDA GREENHOUSE | MAY 30, 2007

WASHINGTON — The Supreme Court on Tuesday made it harder for many workers to sue their employers for discrimination in pay, insisting in a 5-to-4 decision on a tight time frame to file such cases. The dissenters said the ruling ignored workplace realities.

The decision came in a case involving a supervisor at a Goodyear Tire plant in Gadsden, Ala., the only woman among 16 men at the same management level, who was paid less than any of her colleagues, including those with less seniority. She learned that fact late in a career of nearly 20 years — too late, according to the Supreme Court's majority.

The court held on Tuesday that employees may not bring suit under the principal federal anti-discrimination law unless they have filed a formal complaint with a federal agency within 180 days after their pay was set. The timeline applies, according to the decision, even if the effects of the initial discriminatory act were not immediately apparent to the worker and even if they continue to the present day.

From 2001 to 2006, workers brought nearly 40,000 pay discrimination cases. Many such cases are likely to be barred by the court's interpretation of the requirement in Title VII of the Civil Rights Act of 1964 that employees make their charge within 180 days "after the alleged unlawful employment practice occurred."

Workplace experts said the ruling would have broad ramifications and would narrow the legal options of many employees.

In an opinion by Justice Samuel A. Alito Jr., the majority rejected the view of the federal agency, the Equal Employment Opportunity Commission, that each paycheck that reflects the initial discrimination is itself a discriminatory act that resets the clock on the 180-day period, under a rule known as "paycheck accrual."

"Current effects alone cannot breathe life into prior, uncharged discrimination," Justice Alito said in an opinion joined by Chief Justice John G. Roberts Jr. and Justices Antonin Scalia, Anthony M. Kennedy and Clarence Thomas. Justice Thomas once headed the employment commission, the chief enforcer of workers' rights under the statute at issue in this case, usually referred to simply as Title VII.

Under its longstanding interpretation of the statute, the commission actively supported the plaintiff, Lilly M. Ledbetter, in the lower courts. But after the Supreme Court agreed to hear the case last June, the Bush administration disavowed the agency's position and filed a brief on the side of the employer.

In a vigorous dissenting opinion that she read from the bench, Justice Ruth Bader Ginsburg said the majority opinion "overlooks common characteristics of pay discrimination." She said that given the secrecy in most workplaces about salaries, many employees would have no idea within 180 days that they had received a lower raise than others.

An initial disparity, even if known to the employee, might be small, Justice Ginsburg said, leading an employee, particularly a woman or a member of a minority group "trying to succeed in a nontraditional environment" to avoid "making waves." Justice Ginsburg noted that even a small differential "will expand exponentially over an employee's working life if raises are set as a percentage of prior pay."

Justices John Paul Stevens, David H. Souter and Stephen G. Breyer joined the dissent.

Ms. Ledbetter's salary was initially the same as that of her male colleagues. But over time, as she received smaller raises, a substantial disparity grew. By the time she brought suit in 1998, her salary fell short by as much as 40 percent; she was making $3,727 a month, while the lowest-paid man was making $4,286.

A jury in Federal District Court in Birmingham, Ala., awarded her more than $3 million in back pay and compensatory and punitive damages, which the trial judge reduced to $360,000. But the United States Court of Appeals for the 11th Circuit, in Atlanta, erased the verdict entirely, ruling that because Ms. Ledbetter could not show that she was the victim of intentional discrimination during the 180 days before she filed her complaint, she had not suffered an "unlawful employment practice" to which Title VII applied.

Several other federal appeals courts had accepted the employment commission's more relaxed view of the 180-day requirement. The justices accepted Ms. Ledbetter's appeal, Ledbetter v. Goodyear Tire and Rubber Company, No. 05-1074, to resolve the conflict.

Title VII's prohibition of workplace discrimination applies not just to pay but also to specific actions like refusal to hire or promote, denial of a desired transfer and dismissal. Justice Ginsburg argued in her dissenting opinion that while these "singular discrete acts" are readily apparent to an employee who can then make a timely complaint, pay discrimination often presents a more ambiguous picture. She said the court should treat a pay claim as it treated a claim for a "hostile work environment" in a 2002 decision, permitting a charge to be filed "based on the cumulative effect of individual acts."

In response, Justice Alito dismissed this as a "policy argument" with "no support in the statute."

As with an abortion ruling last month, this decision showed the impact of Justice Alito's presence on the court. Justice Sandra Day O'Connor, whom he succeeded, would almost certainly have voted the other way, bringing the opposite outcome.

The impact of the decision on women may be somewhat limited by the availability of another federal law against sex discrimination in the workplace, the Equal Pay Act, which does not contain the 180-day requirement. Ms. Ledbetter initially included an Equal Pay Act complaint, but did not pursue it. That law has additional procedural hurdles and a low damage cap that excludes punitive damages. It does not cover discrimination on the basis of race or Title VII's other protected categories.

In her opinion, Justice Ginsburg invited Congress to overturn the decision, as it did 15 years ago with a series of Supreme Court rulings on civil rights. "Once again, the ball is in Congress's court," she said. Within hours, Senator Hillary Rodham Clinton of New York, who is seeking the Democratic nomination, announced her intention to submit such a bill.

Obama Signs Equal-Pay Legislation

BY SHERYL GAY STOLBERG | JAN. 29, 2009

WASHINGTON — President Obama signed his first bill into law on Thursday, approving equal-pay legislation that he said would "send a clear message that making our economy work means making sure it works for everybody."

Mr. Obama was surrounded by a group of beaming lawmakers, most but not all of them Democrats, in the East Room of the White House as he affixed his signature to the Lilly Ledbetter Fair Pay Act, a law named for an Alabama woman who at the end of a 19-year career as a supervisor in a tire factory complained that she had been paid less than men.

After a Supreme Court ruling against her, Congress approved the legislation that expands workers' rights to sue in this kind of case, relaxing the statute of limitations.

"It is fitting that with the very first bill I sign — the Lilly Ledbetter Fair Pay Act — we are upholding one of this nation's first principles: that we are all created equal and each deserve a chance to pursue our own version of happiness," the president said.

He said he was signing the bill not only in honor of Ms. Ledbetter — who stood behind him, shaking her head and clasping her hands in seeming disbelief — but in honor of his own grandmother, "who worked in a bank all her life, and even after she hit that glass ceiling, kept getting up again" and for his daughters, "because I want them to grow up in a nation that values their contributions, where there are no limits to their dreams."

The ceremony, and a reception afterward in the State Dining Room of the White House, had a celebratory feel. The East Room was packed with advocates for civil rights and workers rights; the legislators, who included House and Senate leaders and two moderate Republicans — Senators Susan Collins and Olympia Snowe, both of Maine — shook Mr. Obama's hand effusively (some, including House Speaker Nancy

President Obama signed his first bill into law on Thursday, approving the Lilly Ledbetter Fair Pay Act, a law named for Ms. Ledbetter, present at the signing, an Alabama woman who at the end of a 19-year career as a supervisor in a tire factory complained that she had been paid less than men.

Pelosi, received presidential pecks on the cheek) as he took the stage. They looked over his shoulder, practically glowing, as Mr. Obama signed his name to the bill, using one pen for each letter.

"I've been practicing signing my name very slowly," Mr. Obama said wryly, looking at a bank of pens before him. He handed the first pen to the bill's chief sponsor, Senator Barbara Mikulski, Democrat of Maryland, and the last to Ms. Ledbetter.

The ceremony also marked First Lady Michelle Obama's policy debut; she spoke afterward in a reception in the State Dining Room, where she called Ms. Ledbetter "one of my favorite people."

Mr. Obama told Ms. Ledbetter's story over and over again during his campaign for the White House; she spoke frequently as an advocate for him during his campaign, and made an appearance at the Democratic National Convention in Denver.

Now 70, Ms. Ledbetter discovered when she was nearing retirement that her male colleagues were earning much more than she was. A jury found her employer, the Goodyear Tire and Rubber Company plant in Gadsden, Ala., guilty of pay discrimination. But in a 5-4 decision, the Supreme Court threw out the case, ruling that she should have filed her suit within 180 days of the date that Goodyear first paid her less than her peers.

Congress tried to pass a law that would have effectively overturned the decision while President George W. Bush was still in office, but the White House opposed the bill; opponents contended it would encourage lawsuits and argued that employees could delay filing their claims in the hope of reaping bigger rewards. But the new Congress passed the bill, which restarts the six-month clock every time the worker receives a paycheck .

Ms. Ledbetter will not see any money as a result of the legislation Mr. Obama signed into law. But what she has gotten, aside from celebrity, is personal satisfaction, as she said in the State Dining Room after the signing ceremony.

"Goodyear will never have to pay me what it cheated me out of," she said. "In fact, I will never see a cent. But with the president's signature today I have an even richer reward."

Obama Moves to Expand Rules Aimed at Closing Gender Pay Gap

BY JULIE HIRSCHFELD DAVIS | JAN. 29, 2016

WASHINGTON — President Obama on Friday moved to require companies to report to the federal government what they pay employees by race, gender and ethnicity, part of his push to crack down on firms that pay women less for doing the same work as men.

"Women are not getting the fair shot that we believe every single American deserves," Mr. Obama said in announcing the proposal, timed to coincide with the seventh anniversary of his signing of the Lilly Ledbetter Fair Pay Act, which makes it easier for people to challenge discriminatory pay. "What kind of example does paying women less set for our sons and daughters?"

The new rules, Mr. Obama's latest bid to use his executive power to address a priority of his that Congress has resisted acting on, would mandate that companies with 100 employees or more include salary information on a form they already submit annually that reports employees' sex, age and job groups.

"Too often, pay discrimination goes undetected because of a lack of accurate information about what people are paid," said Jenny Yang, the chairwoman of the Equal Employment Opportunity Commission, which will publish the proposed regulation jointly with the Department of Labor. "We will be using the information that we're collecting as one piece of information that can inform our investigations."

The requirement would expand on an executive order Mr. Obama issued nearly two years ago that called for federal contractors to submit salary information for women and men. Ms. Yang said the rules would be completed in September, with the first reports due a year later.

"Bridging the stubborn pay gap between men and women in the work force has proven to be very challenging," said Valerie Jarrett, a

President Obama at the White House on Friday after speaking on the seventh anniversary of his signing of the Lilly Ledbetter Fair Pay Act.

senior adviser to Mr. Obama, noting that the median wage for women amounts to 79 percent of that for men. "We have seen progress, but it isn't enough."

White House officials said that the requirement was intended to bolster the government's ability to penalize companies that engage in discriminatory pay practices and to encourage businesses to police themselves better and correct such disparities.

Marc Benioff, the chief executive of Salesforce.com, whom the White House enlisted to help make its case for the rules, said that while he "never intended" to pay women less than men, he had discovered that his company was doing so after two female employees approached him about it.

"We're never going to solve this issue of pay inequality if C.E.O.s like myself and others continue to turn a blind eye to what's happening in their own corporations," Mr. Benioff said in a conference call organized by the White House, adding that he was spending $3 million to close the pay gap at his firm.

Mr. Obama on Friday also renewed his call for Congress to pass a measure allowing women to sue for punitive damages for pay discrimination. Republicans have repeatedly blocked such legislation, arguing that it would lead to frivolous lawsuits.

Republicans have sharply criticized Mr. Obama's moves on pay equity, saying that gender discrimination is already illegal and that additional steps are not necessary.

CHAPTER 2

The Pay Gap Across Industries

Studies have shown that the gender pay gap is felt in nearly every industry in America, affecting women up and down the economic spectrum. As it has become more public, the pay gap has also become a target for workers and executives seeking reform. The articles in this chapter demonstrate the impact of the wage disparity on the lives of women in various industries and income brackets, ranging from Hollywood actresses and sports stars to doctors, nurses and lawyers.

A 44% Pay Divide for Female and Male Law Partners, Survey Says

BY ELIZABETH OLSON | OCT. 12, 2016

AT BIG AMERICAN law firms, there is a 44 percent difference in pay between female partners and their male colleagues, largely because men bring in more big-ticket legal cases, or are better at getting credit for doing so.

Female partners earned an average of $659,000 annually compared with an average of $949,000 for male partners, according to the latest survey of big-firm partners released on Wednesday by the legal search firm Major, Lindsey & Africa.

The survey, which queried 2,100 partners at law firms nationwide, found that average compensation for partners over all was $877,000, which was 22 percent higher than two years ago.

Rebecca Geller, center, with other members of her firm, the Geller Law Group, in Fairfax, Va.

Although billing rates are up across the legal industry, female partners still take home thinner paychecks because, it appears, men are better at receiving credit for landing big cases, according the survey, the fourth in six years.

"We asked partners to pinpoint the factors underlying the pay differences," said Jeffrey A. Lowe, who heads Major, Lindsey's law firm business, "and the No. 1 factor was origination," or who receives credit for bringing a legal matter to the firm.

Rainmaking, or attracting legal work from clients, has always been a top factor in lawyer earning power, and is continuing to grow. The average origination amount, according to the survey, was almost $2.5 million, and that amount was up 25 percent from two years ago. Typically, lawyers' annual compensation is tied to the amount of business they bring.

"We found that, predominantly, a partner's compensation is tied to bringing in business to the law firm," Mr. Lowe said.

Women partners, the report found, brought in an average of $1.7 million worth of business compared with the $2.6 million average of their male counterparts. Because there are more male partners, the average skews higher than if there were equal gender representation. Two years ago, women brought in $1.2 million worth of business, and male counterparts chalked up $2.2 million.

The lag in pay for female partners in either attracting business or getting credit for it could stem from several factors. One is that the "old boys network" still has an outsize influence because of connections made in law school or earlier that affect who is hired to handle their corporate legal matters.

Other factors, including the number of hours worked, are secondary in determining a lawyer's annual pay, according to the survey, which was written by Major, Lindsey and conducted by ALM Legal Intelligence, the research arm of The American Lawyer, a legal publication.

Major, Lindsey & Africa's survey has been tracking gender pay differences since 2010. Two years ago, it found that the gender pay gap was even more pronounced than now — at 47 percent. According to the 2014 figures, female partners earned $531,000 compared with the average $779,000 that their male counterparts were paid.

The amount of business originated increased 6 percent over all from 2010 to 2014, but the earnings seem to be distributed more broadly. The average compensation of white partners rose 14 percent in this year's survey, compared with 2014, to $876,000. The compensation of Hispanic partners increased 100 percent, to $956,000. The compensation of African-American partners rose 39 percent, to $797,000, while that of partners of Asian-Pacific backgrounds increased 36 percent, to $875,000.

The partners who fared the worst in terms of compensation were those who practiced labor and employment law. They earned the lowest average compensation, $597,000. That compared with partners handling corporate work, who earned an average of $1.1 million annually.

Study Finds a Gender Gap at the Top Museums

BY HILARIE M. SHEETS | MARCH 7, 2014

WOMEN RUN JUST A QUARTER of the biggest art museums in the United States and Canada, and they earn about a third less than their male counterparts, according to a report released on Friday by the Association of Art Museum Directors, a professional organization.

The group examined salary data on the 217 members it had last year through the prism of gender, for the first time. The report noted strides made by women at small and midsize museums, with budgets under $15 million, often university or contemporary-art institutions. Here, women have basically achieved parity, holding nearly half of the directorships and earning just about the same as men. But the gap is glaring at big institutions, those with budgets over $15 million: Only 24 percent are led by women, and they make 29 percent less than their male peers.

And just five of the 33 most prominent art museums — those with budgets greater than $20 million — have women at the helm.

"There is a difference if a woman is running one of these big museums," said Elizabeth Easton, director of the Center for Curatorial Leadership, a training program in New York that has helped place nine women in directorships, but none at the country's most influential museums. "Those directors are the most loud and authoritative voices. It sets the tone."

She added: "Everyone just claps their hands and says that it's getting better. But with boards full of men and search committees gravitating to men, it's not going to get better."

Christine Anagnos, director of the association and one of four authors of the report, pointed to a trend of high-profile appointments of men at major museums, replacing female directors, including in Philadelphia, Dallas and Newark.

That trend could change, with the Cleveland Museum of Art searching for a new director; with the announcement last week by Malcolm Rogers that he was retiring from the Museum of Fine Arts, Boston, as soon as a successor is found; and with the directors of the National Gallery in Washington and the Brooklyn Museum being over 65.

But experts debate not only whether women will get those plum jobs, but also whether they will pursue them. "Is it that women are not being offered those jobs, or they're choosing not to take those jobs?" asked Lisa Phillips, director of the New Museum in New York, who initiated the idea for the study.

Written in partnership with the National Center for Arts Research, the report, called "The Gender Gap in Museum Directorships," explores the factors contributing to the gulf at the top and frames the findings within the debate provoked by Sheryl Sandberg's book "Lean In" and Anne-Marie Slaughter's 2012 article "Why Women Still Can't Have It All" in The Atlantic.

Combining large and small institutions, the report found that an average of 42 percent of the association's museum directors were women. That is certainly a different picture from 25 years ago, when only 14 percent of museums in the association were run by women, and a slight improvement from 38 percent five years ago.

On average, however, women who run art institutions earned 21 percent less than their male counterparts in 2013 — a bigger difference than the 18 percent overall median pay split between the sexes reported by the federal Bureau of Labor Statistics.

The report, which incorporated observations from interviews with six executive search recruiters, considered reasons for the gap, including the ratio of men to women on museum boards, which hire directors. While the recruiters agreed that boards were no longer all-male clubs — women now outnumber men, 59 to 30, on the board of the Museum of Fine Arts, Houston, for instance — gender ratios remain uneven. At the Metropolitan Museum of Art, the male voting members still outnumber female ones, 23 to 10. At the National Gallery, the board has seven men and two women.

But Ms. Phillips is skeptical about how much gender composition on a board is a factor in hiring. "We all have biases," she said. "There are many subtle forms of discrimination and self-censorship that are culturally ingrained."

Kimerly Rorschach, a finalist in 2011 to direct the Houston museum, was hired in 2012 to lead the Seattle Art Museum, which has a $23 million budget. She made the leap from director of the Nasher Museum of Art at Duke University, whose budget is under $5 million. Besides Ms. Rorschach, the other four women leading art museum with budgets of over $20 million are Janet Carding at the Royal Ontario Museum, Karol Wight at the Corning Museum of Glass, Nathalie Bondil at the Montreal Museum of Fine Arts and Kaywin Feldman at the Minneapolis Institute of Arts.

"Seattle had an experience of a very successful woman director, and gender wasn't an issue for them," she said, referring to a predecessor, Mimi Gates. "In some of these searches, I think boards can be more focused on outward appearances or the job the person held before than whether they're really bringing the right skills to the job."

Charles Wright, the chairman of the Seattle museum board, which has 39 men and 35 women, said of Ms. Rorschach's compensation: "We're paying what we perceive as top dollar for our current director, and she negotiated well for it. Maybe men historically have had a more inflated sense of themselves and have negotiated harder for compensation than women have."

The skill set for the route up is different from the skill set to be an effective leader, said Kathryn Kolbert, director of the Athena Center for Leadership Studies at Barnard College, which was not involved with the gender gap study. "Many of the skills that women bring are collaboration, working well with boards," she explained. "But women do worse on the visioning factor than men."

Sarah James, of Phillips Oppenheim, an executive recruiter, worked with the Metropolitan Museum, the Guggenheim and the Museum of Fine Arts, Houston, in their last director searches — resulting in the hiring of three men. She said that while women often focused in interviews on how they were great managers, male candidates tended to lead with their ideas and "are very comfortable saying this is what we could do together."

Professional training programs have helped many women move into directorships at midsize museums. Olga Viso, who participated in the Getty Leadership Institute in 2004, is now in her second directorship, at the Walker Art Center in Minneapolis, after leading the Hirshhorn in Washington. Since 2008, the Center for Curatorial Leadership has helped 13 curators become directors, including nine women.

But, of the 13, it was a man, Gary Tinterow, a curator for 28 years at the Metropolitan Museum, who landed the biggest directorship, at the Houston museum, with an operating budget of $52 million.

Kathy Halbreich, a former director of the Walker, questions whether many women actually want to run the big institutions. "Walker was the institution I wanted to lead," said Ms. Halbreich, who chose not to pursue another directorship after her 16-year tenure there, and focuses on curatorial initiatives as associate director of the Museum of Modern Art.

She pointed to three directors and friends — Ann Philbin of the Hammer Museum in Los Angeles, Thelma Golden of the Studio Museum in Harlem, and Ms. Phillips of the New Museum — and said, "Each I know has been approached by bigger institutions, and out of a great sense of mission and self-awareness has decided that where they are is where they're happy."

Ms. James, the recruiter, said she had a difficult time getting women interested in the Guggenheim director's job in 2008, which called for managing its institutions around the globe. "We heard from them that it seemed like an empire," she said. (The job went to Richard Armstrong, former director of the Carnegie Museum of Art.)

But Ms. Phillips, looking across the whole field, now has her doubts about whether women should reject major leadership positions as they open up. "When you see the absence of women," she said, "it makes you wonder whether it's something that we really need to do, regardless of whether we want to do it."

Stubborn Pay Gap Is Found in Nursing

BY CATHERINE SAINT LOUIS | MARCH 24, 2015

MALE NURSES make $5,100 more on average per year than female colleagues in similar positions, researchers reported on Tuesday.

The new analysis, which included data on more than 290,000 registered nurses, also found that the pay gap had not narrowed within workplace settings and specialties from 1988 to 2013. The new study is the first to have measured gender disparities in pay among nurses over time.

"We now have pretty compelling evidence that there are pay inequalities between men and women in nursing over the past 25 years," said Debra J. Barksdale, the director of the doctor of nursing practice program at the University of North Carolina at Chapel Hill, who was not involved with the new study.

Because most nurses are women, "you may think women have caught up or even might be ahead of men, but we find that's not the case," said Ulrike Muench, the lead author of the new study, which was published in JAMA, and an assistant professor of social behavioral sciences at the School of Nursing of the University of California, San Francisco.

The research team, which also included experts at the Yale School of Public Health and Vanderbilt University Medical Center, used data from two surveys. One provided a trove of employment information, like whether nurses worked in hospital or ambulatory settings and the number of years since graduation. But the National Sample Survey of Registered Nurses was discontinued in 2008.

The researchers also relied on census data for information on earnings, finding that the gap "exists and persists in a second nationally representative data set," Dr. Muench said.

The gap varied across specialties, Dr. Muench and her colleagues found. Male cardiology nurses were paid more per year than female colleagues by roughly $6,000 on average. By contrast, male nurses in chronic care — focused on managing conditions like diabetes or asthma — made roughly $3,800 more than women in those specialties.

This new analysis found the pay disparity greatest among nurse anesthetists. About 40 percent are men, and they were paid $17,290 more on average per year than female nurse anesthetists.

The study did not address reasons underpinning the persistent gap. There could be several reasons, Dr. Muench said: Men may be better negotiators, for instance, or perhaps women more often leave the work force to raise children. Women may have a tougher time getting promoted, she said.

"A workplace may offer a bit more to the men in order to diversify," said Diana Mason, a professor of nursing at Hunter College of The City University of New York and former editor of The American Journal of Nursing.

Still, it is possible that women earn less because of a "lingering bias that a man is more of an expert because he's a man," she said.

Amanda Anderson, who has been a critical care nurse for seven years, currently works for Mount Sinai Beth Israel hospital in Manhattan, where nurses are unionized, but she has also worked for other hospitals where nurses are not part of a union.

"I was surprised to read this study, because every time I've changed jobs or gotten an increase in pay, it had to do with my own education or certification," she said.

Ms. Anderson, who recently became a nurse supervisor, said that as a bedside nurse she never thought to ask for a salary increase at any of the four other hospitals she worked at.

She said she had thought nursing salaries were "immune" to a gender gap. "The fact that there is a gender discrepancy even with a system that seems so regimented and some of the time has a labor component is shocking," she said.

National Nurses United, the country's largest union for registered nurses, with 185,000 members, estimates that only about 20 percent of the more than 1.6 million nurses nationwide who work in hospitals are unionized.

Dr. Mason said the new analysis was an opportunity for chief nurse officers to ask their employers for wage data by gender for employees in equal positions with comparable experience in order to root out bias in pay.

Peter McMenamin, a health economist and a spokesman for the American Nurses Association, commended the study. "The folks who did the study are well qualified and they have lots of data," he said. "But my main hesitance in terms of statistics is they have fewer men."

Only 7 to 10 percent of nurses are male, he acknowledged. But with a smaller sample, he said, "the reliability of the answers is less robust."

"You can't say this is all a statistical fluke," he added. "It's not. But there are different things that could explain some of this challenge."

Next, the researchers aim to focus on explanations for earning gaps in nursing.

Dr. Paid Less: An Old Title
Still Fits Female Physicians

BY CATHERINE SAINT LOUIS | JULY 11, 2016

FEMALE PHYSICIANS at some of the nation's most prominent public medical schools earn nearly $20,000 less a year on average than their male colleagues, according to an analysis published on Monday in JAMA Internal Medicine.

Before adjusting for factors that could influence income, the researchers found that the absolute difference between the genders was more than $51,000 a year.

Several studies have found a persistent pay gap between male and female doctors. But those reports relied mostly on doctors reporting their own incomes, or focused on pay disparities in one specialty or one region, or on starting salaries.

The new study draws on salary information from a much larger, objective sample. The researchers went to great lengths to account for a variety of factors that can influence income, such as the volume of patients seen by a physician and the number of publications he or she had written.

Medical professionals greeted the results with exasperation.

"It's 2016, and yet in a very methodically strong, large study that covers a broad swath of the country, you're still seeing at the very least a 10 percent difference in what men and women take home," said Dr. Molly Cooke, a professor of medicine at University of California, San Francisco, who has studied salary disparities among physicians.

Dr. Vineet M. Arora, an associate professor of medicine at the University of Chicago, wrote an editorial accompanying the study. "This paper is going to make women academic physicians start a conversation with their institutions to promote transparency and gender equality, because at the end of the day, it's not fair," she said in an interview.

The analysis included data on roughly 10,000 physician faculty members at 24 medical schools, including those of the University of North Carolina and the University of Washington. Researchers at Harvard Medical School and Massachusetts General Hospital relied on public databases of employee salaries in 12 states, and data from Doximity, a networking site for physicians, to adjust for factors that can influence income — years since residency, specialty and age, for instance.

Only public medical schools, not private ones, were included, because states like Florida and Texas post employee salaries online.

After adjusting for a variety of factors, the researchers found that female neurosurgeons and cardiothoracic surgeons and women in other surgical subspecialties made roughly $44,000 less than comparable men in those fields.

The average pay gap between female and male orthopedic surgeons was nearly $41,000. The difference was about $38,000 among oncologists and blood specialists, about $36,000 among obstetrician-gynecologists and $34,000 among cardiologists.

Radiology was the only specialty in which women were paid more. Their adjusted average salary exceeded that of male radiologists by roughly $2,000.

Pay differences by gender appeared across all faculty ranks. Full female professors made roughly the same income ($250,971) as male associate professors ($247,212) despite outranking them.

The study's limitations included a lack of information about who was on a tenure track. More important, reported incomes in some states may not include all payments to physicians, but both men and women are likely to have been affected by such an exclusion.

The researchers also found stark variations in the salary gap at different medical schools, suggesting some address pay inequities more aggressively than others.

"The biggest surprise is there are some schools where this doesn't seem to be an issue," said Dr. Anupam B. Jena, the study's lead author and an associate professor of health care policy at Harvard Medical School.

At two medical centers in the West, female physicians were paid roughly $54,000 and $59,000 less, on average, than their male counterparts. At two schools, there was little income difference. Dr. Jena declined to the identify the schools.

"What policies, procedures, leadership or culture at these sites helps to counteract a gender pay gap?" Dr. Arora asked in her editorial.

Dr. Cooke said her salary had been corrected twice by university administrators — once after research she helped conduct revealed pay disparities among physicians in the late 1980s.

She attributes the persistent pay gap partly to the complicated and individualized nature of academic salaries, as well as a lack of transparency.

A subtle bias against women often is a factor, she said, "until a periodic study comes along, where people go, 'Oh, my God, it's happening, again.' "

In the worst cases, the pay gap exists because of "clear discrimination by department chairs in salary settings," Dr. Jena said.

But he also suggested that two other factors mighty play a role. Men and women may negotiate differently, and "male physicians may be more aggressive in terms of obtaining outside salary offers," he said.

"Extremely helpful" research like Dr. Jena's keeps the issue in the public eye, said Dr. Kim Templeton, the president of American Medical Women's Association and a professor of orthopedic surgery at the University of Kansas, which contributed data to the study.

"But just having it out there isn't going to fix the problem."

At Google, Employee-Led Effort Finds Men Are Paid More Than Women

BY DAISUKE WAKABAYASHI | SEPT. 8, 2017

SAN FRANCISCO — Female employees are paid less than male staff members at most job levels within Google, and the pay disparity extends as women climb the corporate ladder, according to data compiled by employees that provide a snapshot of salary information at the internet giant.

A spreadsheet, obtained by The New York Times, contains salary and bonus information for 2017 that was shared by about 1,200 United States Google employees, or about 2 percent of the company's global work force.

While Google said the data painted an incomplete picture of how people are paid, the salary details shared by employees are likely to heighten concerns over gender disparities in Silicon Valley.

Even as America's technology giants continue to grow in wealth and influence, most have shown little progress in leveling the playing field for women, who are underrepresented in key engineering and leadership roles and are paid less than men. These gender imbalances are reflected in long-term studies of large companies around the world by the McKinsey Global Institute.

The scrutiny has been especially intense at Google. Long regarded as one of the world's best workplaces because of its perks and generous compensation, the company is under examination by the Labor Department and has faced criticism from investors and some of its own employees over differences in how women and men are paid.

"Silicon Valley has established itself as the boys' club of the West, just like how Wall Street has established itself as the boys' club of the East," said Natasha Lamb, director of equity research and shareholder engagement at Arjuna Capital, a wealth management firm that takes activist positions on issues such as gender pay.

Employees in Google's offices at Kendall Square in Cambridge, Mass., Aug. 5, 2014. According to a 2017 spreadsheet compiled by employees, there is significant pay disparity between men and women at Google.

At a shareholder meeting for Alphabet, Google's parent company, earlier this year, Arjuna Capital put forward a proposal for the company to disclose what women make compared with their male peers. Arjuna had successfully persuaded seven of nine technology companies, including Apple, Amazon.com and Microsoft, to disclose that data. Alphabet's directors urged shareholders to vote against the measure, and it failed.

The self-reported Google salary spreadsheet was started in 2015 by a former employee who wanted to help co-workers negotiate better salaries. That employees were keeping track of this information became public knowledge soon after, but the spreadsheet's details remained private.

The salary information in the spreadsheet cannot be viewed as an exact portrait of what people make at the company, because some employees may have erred when they put in their information. At some job levels, only a handful of employees volunteered to share their salary information, so a few salaries can skew the data. Even though it's not a random sample of staff members, the information is tracked closely throughout the company.

The spreadsheet covers levels one through six of Google's job hierarchy, from entry-level data center workers at level one to managers and experienced engineers at level six. It does not include company executives and top-level engineers, who receive a wider range of salaries.

At five of the six job levels, women are paid less than men. At level three, the entry level for technical positions, women make 4 percent less than men at $124,000 in salary and bonus. But it widens to 6 percent by the time employees reach midcareer status, around level five, with women earning, on average, $11,000 less than men.

Google said the spreadsheet's information does not take into account a number of factors, like where employees are based, whether they are in higher-paying technical positions, and job performance.

Based upon its own analysis from January, Google said female employees make 99.7 cents for every dollar a man makes, accounting for factors like location, tenure, job role, level and performance.

Google said its analysis includes salary, bonus and equity compensation for 95 percent of employees between levels one and nine — three levels beyond what was reflected in the data shared with The Times — while excluding vice presidents and above. Google did not provide a breakdown of how it arrived at that calculation.

Eileen Naughton, Google's vice president of people operations, said the gender pay disparity reflected in the internal spreadsheet is "not a representative sample" for other, more complex reasons. For example, a person in a nontechnical role may be at the same job level as an engineer, but will be paid significantly less because "there is a premium paid in all markets for highly technical talent."

In its annual diversity report, Google said only 20 percent of its higher-paid technical positions are filled by women, and women make up 31 percent of the company's overall work force.

The percentage of women in technical positions is lower than the overall percentage of female employees, with more women in sales, marketing, human resources or legal. Those roles, according to Ms. Naughton, do not have the same entry-level or midcareer salaries as technical positions.

Other factors include geography and job performance. A position at Google's main office in Mountain View, Calif. — where the cost of living is high — may pay a lot more than a Google employee of a similar rank hired in a cheaper market. In addition, job performance significantly governs a person's pay over time — another factor not reflected in the spreadsheet.

Google said it tries to exclude gender when determining salaries. Human resources analysts who determine what salary a person is offered when he or she joins Google do not know the candidate's gender. Similarly, when an employee's salary is up for annual review, the company takes into account the person's job performance, location and competitive salaries — but the analysts are not informed of the person's gender.

"There's a meme around tech companies and Silicon Valley, around issues having to do with gender equity in tech," Ms. Naughton said. "I do believe Google, because of its size and perhaps our size or our prominence in people's everyday lives, I think we're in the spotlight. It feels a little unfair."

What Google pays men versus women is at the heart of a dispute with the Department of Labor. The company is fighting over how much data it needs to hand over as part of a routine audit of its pay practices. Google is a federal contractor because it sells advertising to the government.

In April, a Labor Department official said in a hearing that it needed more data because "we found systemic compensation disparities against women pretty much across the entire work force." The Labor Department hasn't charged Google with any wrongdoing.

Google said it has already shared a lot of data and documents and that the Labor Department is overreaching by asking for employees' private information. An administrative law judge ruled in July that

Google had to disclose some data but not as much as the Labor Department had wanted.

Google is also confronting broader questions about how women at the company are regarded after a software engineer published a memo arguing that Google's efforts to reach equal representation of women in technology and leadership roles were unfair and not good for business.

James Damore, 28, the engineer who wrote the memo, said the shortage of women in engineering and leadership positions stemmed from what he called "personality differences" between men and women — like a woman having lower stress tolerance. Google fired Mr. Damore last month for "advancing harmful gender stereotypes."

James Finberg, a civil rights lawyer and partner at Altshuler Berzon L.L.P., said he expected to bring a class-action lawsuit against Google for "substantial gender disparities" later this month. Mr. Finberg said more than 90 current and former female employees have come forward to be plaintiffs.

He said that these women spoke about experiencing discrimination by being slotted into positions at a level below a man with similar qualifications and that women are not promoted with the same frequency as men. He said that some of the gender stereotypes cited in the memo are widespread and that they kept women out of higher-paying engineering jobs.

"It is an atmosphere filled with stereotypes, that the comments espoused in the memo were not isolated incidents," Mr. Finberg said. "They are more of the norm than the anomaly."

Roger Federer, $731,000;
Serena Williams, $495,000:
The Pay Gap in Tennis

BY BEN ROTHENBERG | APRIL 12, 2016

DANIEL ISLAND, S.C. — With renewed scrutiny on the disparate compensation paid to male and female athletes after a wage discrimination lawsuit filed by the United States women's soccer team, tennis has been cited as a leader in gender equality among major sports.

But even in tennis, where men and women compete alongside one another at the same stadiums around the world, female players still earn significantly less than their male peers.

Grand Slam tournaments and the handful of other top combined events that pay men and women equally remain the exceptions.

Raymond Moore, the tournament director of the BNP Paribas Open in Indian Wells, Calif., an equal prize money event, resigned last month after saying that WTA players were "lucky" to be able to "ride on the coattails of the men." His comments led to conversations at subsequent tournaments about the financial realities for men and women in tennis.

At the Volvo Car Open in Charleston, S.C., last week, several top players pointed out that the discussion of equal pay often distorts the distinct advantage male players still have in annual compensation.

"The facts were not put on the table; the fact is we don't earn equal prize money," said Andrea Petkovic, a German player ranked 30th. "It's not true. We only earn it in the Grand Slams and a few other tournaments, but men earn more than we do. I think it was discussed in the wrong manner, and that was very sad to see."

Although men and women are compensated more comparably in tennis than in any other major sport, the annual prize money paid to the top 100 earners on the WTA and ATP Tours roughly matches the general pay gap in American workplaces, with female tennis players earning 80 cents on each dollar men earn. The median pay gap between a woman in the top 100 and her opposite number on the men's tour is $120,624.

"I think that sometimes we just hope that those problems are in the past, and that we have come much further," Petkovic said. "But it's good to be confronted with the thoughts of men that still think that way, and it's maybe nice for us to have discussions with them and to explain our point of view.

"I just wish that we would be a leader, that it wouldn't matter about who is more popular, who is this or that. We, as a sport, could stand for something more than equal prize money — we'd stand for community and sportsmanship."

Billie Jean King, who pushed for equality as the women's professional game developed, has remained an advocate for women's issues in sports and many other areas.

"We have a chance to continue to lead," King said of tennis. "To have equal prize money in the majors sends a message. It's not about the money, it's about the message."

That message shines brightest under the sport's biggest spotlights, at the four Grand Slam events, where men and women are paid equally. The United States Open became the first Grand Slam event to offer equal pay, in 1973, and Wimbledon the last, in 2007.

But at other large combined ATP-WTA tournaments, where the men and women are sold together under one ticket, the prize money disparity can be stark. The Western & Southern Open in Mason, Ohio, the biggest event in the weeks before the United States Open, attracts dazzling constellations of top men's and women's stars each year to the fourth-largest tennis tournament in the country.

The tournament, in which the United States Tennis Association owns a majority stake, pays the women only 63 cents on the dollar as compared with the men. Last year, Roger Federer received $731,000 for defending his title at the tournament, while Serena Williams received $495,000 for defending hers hours later.

Organizers cite a technicality in the WTA's structure to justify the pay differential. The tournament is one of nine Masters 1000 events, the top tier on the ATP Tour. But the top tier of the WTA Tour is four Premier Mandatory events, which include tournaments in Miami, Madrid and Indian Wells, where women can expect equal compensation to men. The Ohio event sits in the next tier, the Premier 5.

Women are also paid less than men at similar Premier 5 events in Canada and Rome, which are held in conjunction with men's tournaments. (At all tour events outside the Grand Slams, men and women play best-of-three-set matches.)

Many WTA-only events, including the one now known as the Volvo Car Open, have flourished. Attendance here consistently dwarfs lower-tier ATP events nearby in Atlanta and Winston-Salem, N.C., and it has drawn crowds similar to, or ahead of, the ones at the comparable ATP event in Washington, which added a lower-tier WTA field in 2012. But the total men's purse in Washington is $1,877,705, while the Charleston purse was about $753,000.

"There's no question that we want to lessen that gap — it's our commitment to the players," said Bob Moran, the Volvo Car Open's tournament director.

There are occasional combined events at which a higher-tier WTA event pays a larger purse than its lower-tier ATP counterpart. At the China Open, held in Beijing in October, the men's champion earns 67 percent of the pay earned by the women's champion. But the disparity is steeper at tournaments in which the ATP event is of a higher designation. In Rio de Janeiro in February, the men's champion, Pablo Cuevas, won $303,300, more than seven times the $43,000 paid to the women's champion, Francesca Schiavone.

The pay gap extends all the way down the ladder on the ATP and WTA tours. According to a 2014 study by the International Tennis Federation that analyzed the average costs for playing professional tennis and the prize money from the previous year, 336 male players could earn enough to cover average expenses, while only 253 women could.

Prize money is generated from each tournament's sponsors, television rights deals, ticket sales and other on-site concessions. The total revenue of the ATP and WTA tours has fluctuated, with a gap of $2.6 million in 2008 giving way to a men's advantage of $37.4 million in 2014.

To capitalize on the popularity of superstars like Federer, Novak Djokovic and Rafael Nadal, the ATP Tour in recent years has gained significant increases in prize money, and those increases have benefited women in equal-pay events. That does not please everyone in the sport.

Sergiy Stakhovsky, a member of the ATP Player Council, said he wanted to see a moratorium on adding combined events to allow the men's game — "a different product, which is better" — to stand on its own. Stakhovsky, ranked 111th, bristles at the blowback combined tournaments receive when they do not offer equal pay.

"That's the only reason why we don't want them is because it's always going to come one way or another that we're the bad guys," Stakhovsky said. "This way, we have our own venue, they have their own venue. I think that women deserve to be paid more. I'm not saying they deserve to be paid less. But this has nothing to do with paying us.

"We've been through a lot of talks with the Grand Slams in the last three years, and the increases have been significant and we're very grateful," Stakhovsky added. "But every time we came to the table, and every time there was a number we asked for, we got half of it. And we know why."

The top-ranked Djokovic was criticized at Indian Wells for saying men "should get awarded more" because "the stats are showing that we have much more spectators."

Some ATP players, most notably Andy Murray, have been outspoken advocates for equal pay for women. But the American player Madison Keys said that many of the male players she knows "freak out and make it seem like every single week we get the same — which is not true."

"I feel like it's one of those conversations: When you're friends with someone, you don't talk about politics; when you're friends with someone, you don't talk about equal prize money in tennis," she added.

Top Female Players Accuse U.S. Soccer of Wage Discrimination

BY ANDREW DAS | MARCH 31, 2016

U.S. SOCCER, the governing body for the sport in America, pays the members of the men's and women's national teams who represent the United States in international competitions. The men's team has historically been mediocre. The women's team has been a quadrennial phenomenon, winning world and Olympic championships and bringing much of the country to a standstill in the process.

Citing this disparity, as well as rising revenue numbers, five players on the women's team filed a federal complaint Wednesday, accusing U.S. Soccer of wage discrimination because, they said, they earned as little as 40 percent of what players on the United States men's national team earned even as they marched to the team's third World Cup championship last year. The five players, some of the world's most prominent women's athletes, said they were being shortchanged on everything from bonuses to appearance fees to per diems.

The case, submitted to the Equal Employment Opportunity Commission, the federal agency that enforces civil rights laws against workplace discrimination, is the latest front in the spreading debate over equal treatment of female athletes. A tennis tournament director was forced to resign recently after saying that female players "ride on the coattails of the men," and the N.C.A.A. has drawn scrutiny for the financial disparities between the men's and women's basketball tournaments.

"The numbers speak for themselves," said goalkeeper Hope Solo, one of the players to sign the complaint. "We are the best in the world, have three World Cup championships, four Olympic championships." Solo said the men's players "get paid more to just show up than we get paid to win major championships."

Solo was joined in the complaint by the co-captains Carli Lloyd and Becky Sauerbrunn, forward Alex Morgan and midfielder Megan Rapinoe.

With Carli Lloyd and Megan Rapinoe out front, and Mayor Bill de Blasio behind, members of the U.S. women's soccer team make their way down the Canyon of Heroes during a July 2015 New York City parade in their honor for winning the World Cup.

U.S. Soccer officials pushed back forcefully on the players' claims in a conference call Thursday night, citing figures that the federation said showed the men's national team produced revenue and attendance about double that of the women's team, and television ratings that were "a multiple" of what the women attract, according to Sunil Gulati, the U.S. Soccer president. A federation spokesman, Neil Buethe, called some of the revenue figures in the players' complaint "inaccurate, misleading or both."

In a statement released earlier Thursday, U.S. Soccer recounted the role the federation has played in the growth of women's soccer, including its introduction to the Olympic Games and in providing full-time salaries for top players. It said it was willing to discuss compensation as part of continuing talks over a new collective bargaining agreement.

But in linking their compensation to the men's pay, the women's players put U.S. Soccer in a difficult position. The federation has collective bargaining agreements with both teams, but the financial terms differ widely.

A men's player, for example, receives $5,000 for a loss in a friendly match but as much as $17,625 for a win against a top opponent. A women's player receives $1,350 for a similar match, but only if the United States wins; women's players receive no bonuses for losses or ties.

Opportunities for women to participate in sports have increased greatly in the more than 40 years since the passage of the gender-equity legislation known as Title IX. But sports officials continue to struggle with matters of compensation.

It has been argued that men's sports, and their players, deserve a financial edge because they draw bigger crowds and generate far more money in ticket sales and corporate sponsorships. That is the case for U.S. Soccer's national teams, the federation said Thursday. But that is not true for every sport. Women's figure skating, for instance, has often drawn higher TV ratings and bigger crowds than men's figure skating.

In their complaint, the five players cited recent U.S. Soccer financial reports as proof that they have become the federation's main economic engine even as, they said, they often earned only half as much — or less — than their male counterparts.

At the same time, the players said, they exceeded revenue projections by as much as $16 million in 2015, when their World Cup triumph set television viewership records and a nine-game victory tour in packed stadiums produced record gate receipts and attendance figures.

U.S. Soccer officials disputed those figures, arguing that the women and their lawyer, Jeffrey Kessler, cherry-picked an extraordinarily successful year to draw broad conclusions.

Michael LeRoy, who teaches collective bargaining and sports at the University of Illinois, said that market conditions between the men's and women's sports are vastly different. LeRoy pointed to a high-profile case brought by Marianne Stanley, the women's basketball coach at the University of Southern California in the early 1990s, who argued she should be paid at a level equal to the men's coach. Her legal effort was unsuccessful.

"They have to prove equality of work and market conditions, and it's such a rigid legal requirement," LeRoy said of the women's soccer players.

While women have often been dismissed in international soccer — the men's World Cup began in 1930 and the women's not until 1991 — they have become the sport's standard-bearers in the United States. The women's team has provided the type of repeated success that has remained elusive for the American men. Not so long ago, a woman, Mia Hamm, may have been the best-known soccer player in the country.

When Hamm and her teammates won the 1999 World Cup in the United States, they also set records for attendance and television viewing. Last summer, when the United States defeated Japan to win another Women's World Cup, the final was seen by 25.4 million viewers on Fox — a record for a men's or women's soccer game on English-language television in this country.

"We have been quite patient over the years with the belief that the federation would do the right thing and compensate us fairly," said Lloyd, the most valuable player of the Women's World Cup.

Although only five players signed the complaint, they said they were acting on behalf of the entire women's team, saying they are all employees of U.S. Soccer through their national team contracts. That is significant, according to Peter Romer-Friedman, the deputy director of litigation for the Washington Lawyers' Committee for Civil Rights.

"By speaking up publicly, the players are saying, 'It's important for the public to know that we've filed this suit,' " Romer-Friedman said. "Frankly, as a civil rights lawyer, it is important for them to speak out because it has an educational effect."

The filing of the complaint was the latest move in an increasingly contentious legal fight between U.S. Soccer and the women's national team, which is favored to repeat as Olympic champion at the Rio

Games in August but has long grumbled about its pay, working conditions and travel and hotel arrangements.

The long-simmering feud boiled over after last summer's Women's World Cup triumph. A match in Hawaii that was part of the team's victory tour was canceled when the players refused to play on an artificial-turf field they deemed unsafe. Gulati later apologized for the situation.

Two months later, the disagreement veered into federal court when U.S. Soccer took the unusual step of filing a lawsuit against the national team's players' union as part of a dispute about the validity of the players' collective bargaining agreement. The federation contends the agreement, which expired in 2012, lives on in a memorandum of understanding the sides signed in early 2013. The union contends it does not.

In response to the complaint filed Wednesday, U.S. Soccer argued that not only was the players' pay collectively bargained, but that the players had insisted more than once on a salary-based system as a means of economic security over the bonus-centric plan the men work under. Russell Sauer, the outside counsel for the federation during labor talks, also said the women's labor contract included provisions — severance and injury pay, health benefits and maternity leave, for example — not available to the men's team.

"The truth is," Sauer said, "the players are claiming discrimination based on a more conservative structure, based on guaranteed compensation rather than pay to play, which they themselves requested, negotiated and approved of not once, but twice."

Furthermore, U.S. Soccer noted, a major source of revenue and contention — World Cup prize money — is determined by FIFA, world soccer's governing body, not the federation. But the women's complaint seems to take aim at a bigger share of domestic revenue, like sponsorships and television contracts, and U.S. Soccer financial reports hint at a richer future involving the team: The federation's budget projections for 2016 include $2.3 million for a 10-game victory tour after this summer's Olympics.

Carli Lloyd: Why I'm Fighting for Equal Pay

ESSAY | BY CARLI LLOYD | APRIL 10, 2016

I'VE WORN A U.S. Soccer uniform for 12 years and have done so proudly. I've had some of the greatest moments of my life — winning two Olympic gold medals and the 2015 Women's World Cup — wearing that uniform. So when I joined four teammates in filing a wage-discrimination complaint against U.S. Soccer late last month, it had nothing to do with how much I love to play for my country.

It had everything to do with what's right and what's fair, and with upholding a fundamental American concept: equal pay for equal play.

Even if you are female.

Simply put, we're sick of being treated like second-class citizens. It wears on you after a while. And we are done with it.

The United States women's national team is the most successful team in the history of U.S. Soccer. We've won three World Cups and will try to win our fifth Olympic gold medal this summer in Brazil. When we captured the Women's World Cup title in Canada in July, we drew the highest American television rating for soccer in history and, according to a financial report published by U.S. Soccer last month, helped generate $17.7 million in profit for the federation.

Yet even though U.S. Soccer's financials confirm that we are the driving force that generates a majority of the revenue for the federation, when we as a team presented our proposal for increased compensation in our new collective bargaining agreement, U.S. Soccer told us, on more than one occasion, that our proposal was not rational. Essentially, the federation said that it had a certain sum of money set aside for the women's team and that our proposal was unacceptable.

We've gotten nowhere negotiating with our federation for years, and it became clear to us that nothing had changed. That's why we went to the Equal Employment Opportunity Commission with our complaint.

I won't bury you with numbers, but there are a few important basic facts worth noting. Each year, the United States men's and women's national teams each play a minimum of 20 friendly matches. The top five players on the men's team make an average of $406,000 each year from these games. The top five women are guaranteed only $72,000 each year.

Yes, U.S. Soccer has stepped up to support the National Women's Soccer League — it also subsidizes our salaries for the N.W.S.L., at roughly $54,000 per player — and yes, we can get some modest bonuses by playing for the national team. But still, the inequality is jarring.

If I were a male soccer player who won a World Cup for the United States, my bonus would be $390,000. Because I am a female soccer player, the bonus I got for our World Cup victory last summer was $75,000.

The men get almost $69,000 for making a World Cup roster. As women, we get $15,000 for making the World Cup team.

I understand that the men's World Cup generates vastly more money globally than the women's event, but the simple truth is that U.S. Soccer projects that our team will generate a profit of $5.2 million in 2017 while the men are forecast to lose almost $1 million. Yet we get shortchanged coming and going.

I was on the road for about 260 days last year. When I am traveling internationally, I get $60 a day for expenses. Michael Bradley gets $75. Maybe they figure that women are smaller and thus eat less.

When Hope Solo or Alex Morgan, say, makes a sponsor appearance for U.S. Soccer, she gets $3,000. When Geoff Cameron or Jermaine Jones makes the same sort of appearance, he gets $3,750.

Our beef is not with the men's national team; we love those guys, and we support those guys. It's with the federation, and its history of treating us as if we should be happy that we are professional players and not working in the kitchen or scrubbing the locker room.

The fact that women are being mistreated financially is, sadly, not a breaking news story. It goes on in every field. We can't right all the world's wrongs, but we're totally determined to right the unfairness in our field, not just for ourselves but for the young players coming up behind us and for our soccer sisters around the world.

The Matildas — Australia's women's national team, which is currently ranked fifth in the world — have battled their federation for years and went on strike last year over the federation's refusal to pay the players more than $21,000 a year. The women on the Colombian national team recently went four months without being paid at all.

When I first made the national team, there were no salaries and no health benefits, so yes, we've made some progress. But we're nowhere near where we should be.

I don't think anyone would say that the women on the United States national team are not great role models and ambassadors. Everywhere we go, we connect with fans, sign autographs and represent our sport and federation with class. We will continue to do that, provided that U.S. Soccer treats us in the same manner.

Two years ago, before the Algarve Cup, an important annual tournament in Portugal, we considered going on strike over these issues, but we weren't completely united then and wound up backing down.

We are not backing down anymore.

If I've learned anything in my career, it's that nothing worthwhile in life comes easy. That's just the way it is. This isn't about a money grab. It's about doing the right thing, the fair thing. It's about treating people the way they deserve to be treated, no matter their gender.

CARLI LLOYD is a co-captain of the United States women's national team and the author of a forthcoming memoir, "When Nobody Was Watching."

Catt Sadler Leaves E! Entertainment, Saying a Male Co-Host Earned Twice as Much

BY MAGGIE ASTOR | DEC. 20, 2017

CATT SADLER said it was her dream job. After 12 years at E! Entertainment, she was a co-host of two shows, "Daily Pop" during the day and the network's flagship "E! News" at night.

But on Tuesday, she signed off for the last time because, she said, the company was paying her half as much as her male "E! News" co-host, Jason Kennedy.

Neither Ms. Sadler nor E! would disclose specific salary figures. Ms. Sadler said in an interview on Wednesday that in early 2017, a friend who is an executive at the network informed her of the disparity.

Once it came time to negotiate a new contract, she demanded to be paid comparably.

When the company refused, she decided she could not stay, she said.

"It's heartbreaking in one sense, but I believe that you have to act in alignment with your beliefs," Ms. Sadler said. "As much as I wanted to stay, I do know my worth, I do know the inner workings of the network, and I just wanted what was fair and reasonable."

The network, which is owned by NBC, rejected the allegation that it paid Ms. Sadler less because she is a woman, saying in a statement that it "compensates employees fairly and appropriately based on their roles, regardless of gender."

An E! spokeswoman said Ms. Sadler's and Mr. Kennedy's roles were not comparable.

In addition to co-hosting "E! News" five nights a week, Mr. Kennedy co-hosts "Live From the Red Carpet," one of the network's most lucrative programs, while Ms. Sadler was one of three hosts of "Daily Pop" and co-hosted "E! News" twice a week, the spokeswoman said. ("Live From the Red Carpet" airs before major awards shows like the

Academy Awards and the Grammy Awards, not year-round.)

Ms. Sadler said she had taken on substantial new responsibilities when "Daily Pop" was introduced. For several months, she co-hosted both "Daily Pop" and "E! News" five days a week. She eventually cut back on her "E! News" duties because of the strain of doing both every day. Even after that, she said, she was hosting seven shows a week to Mr. Kennedy's five.

"I inherited a lot more work and several more work hours, and I did all of that all year long without a single extra dime," she said. "I did that in good faith because I'm a team player and I wanted both shows to succeed. I trusted that, come time to renegotiate, I would be compensated fairly for all of that work moving forward."

Mr. Kennedy's representatives did not respond to phone calls on Wednesday. Before Ms. Sadler's final show, he tweeted that he would miss her but did not mention the pay issue.

After Ms. Sadler posted an explanation of her decision online, she received an outpouring of support, including from the actresses Jessica Chastain and Olivia Munn, and the former "E! News" host Maria Menounos.

"I know this wasn't easy," Ms. Menounos wrote. "Good for you."

On average, American women make 80 cents for every dollar men make. Just two months ago, in a case similar to Ms. Sadler's, the Australian television host Lisa Wilkinson quit her job after unsuccessful contract negotiations. Australian newspapers reported that her co-host, Karl Stefanovic, was paid nearly twice as much.

Ms. Sadler said she hoped her decision would encourage other women to demand equal pay. As for her own future, she said she would love to host a show that would foster "discussions about this very topic."

Acknowledging the support of Ms. Chastain, Ms. Munn and others, she said, "If these women celebrities and non-celebrities alike want to have these conversations on a huge scale for the world to watch and there can be some element of change that comes as a response to that, then that's the kind of TV I would love to make."

Emma Stone Says Male Co-Stars Cut Their Own Salaries to Tackle Inequity

BY SOPHIE HAIGNEY | JULY 7, 2017

EMMA STONE has become the latest woman in Hollywood to speak out about gender pay inequality, saying that some of her male co-stars have taken cuts to level the gap between their wages.

"In my career so far, I've needed my male co-stars to take a pay cut so that I may have parity with them," Ms. Stone said in a conversation with Billie Jean King, the former professional tennis player, published by Out Magazine on Thursday. "And that's something they do for me because they feel it's what's right and fair."

Such paycheck concessions from men helped Ms. Stone get paid more for future films, she explained. "If my male co-star, who has a higher quote than me but believes we are equal, takes a pay cut so that I can match him, that changes my quote in the future and changes my life," she said.

It was not clear which male co-stars she was referring to. Ms. Stone's publicist did not immediately respond to a request for comment.

Ms. Stone, who won the Academy Award for best actress this year for "La La Land," and also played major roles in "Birdman," "The Help," and the "Amazing Spider-Man" movies, is currently promoting "The Battle of the Sexes," a new film based on a 1973 tennis match between Ms. King and a male tennis player, Bobby Riggs. Ms. King was a pioneer in fighting for gender-pay parity; she lobbied the U.S. Open vigorously about the disparity between women's and men's prize money. The movie will be released in September.

Emphasizing that Ms. King's story remained relevant today, Ms. Stone said, "I go more to the blanket issue that women, in general, are making four-fifths at best." Ms. King interjected: "White women. If you're African-American or Hispanic it goes down, and then Asian-Americans make 90 cents to the dollar."

In the United States in 2016, women's median weekly full-time earnings were 81.9 percent of men's median weekly earnings. For Hispanic women in comparison with white men, that figure was 57.2 percent, and for black women compared with white men it was 62.5 percent.

It's difficult to determine the precise wage gap for Hollywood in particular. As Ms. Stone noted in the interview, factors including the relative sizes of roles, box-office sales, and genre of films make it hard to compare salaries across genders in the industry. Still, it's clear that many big-budget female stars make less than their male counterparts. One 2014 study showed that female stars' average earnings per film increase until they turn 34 and then decrease rapidly; meanwhile, male stars' average earnings per film increase until they turn 51 and then remain stable.

Other stars have spoken up about this: Jennifer Lawrence wrote an essay in 2015 when leaked documents showed she was paid less than her co-star Bradley Cooper in "American Hustle." Amy Adams, another of the co-stars in that movie, has also spoken out as well.

In some cases, and as Ms. Lawrence suggested in her essay, stars propose that the solution is for women to negotiate more aggressively. This notion — also made popular in business circles by Sheryl Sandberg's book "Lean In" — has been criticized both for its failure to address the wage gap on a systemic level or to be a real recourse for women who aren't already in positions of economic power.

Efforts to reach several co-stars through their publicists were unsuccessful on Friday.

Mark Wahlberg and Agency Will Donate $2 Million to Time's Up After Outcry Over Pay

BY JEFFERY C. MAYS | JAN. 13, 2018

MARK WAHLBERG and his talent agency, William Morris Endeavor, will donate $2 million to a fund dedicated to fighting pay inequity and harassment of women in Hollywood.

The donation will be made in the name of Michelle Williams, Mr. Wahlberg's co-star in the movie "All the Money in the World," after an outcry about pay discrepancy in reshoots for the film. Ms. Williams received a per diem of $80 for 10 days of work while Mr. Wahlberg negotiated a fee of $1.5 million. The two actors are represented by the same agency.

"Over the last few days my reshoot fee for 'All the Money in the World' has become an important topic of conversation," Mr. Wahlberg said in a statement. "I 100% support the fight for fair pay and I'm donating the $1.5M to the Time's Up Legal Defense Fund in Michelle Williams' name."

Through a spokeswoman, Mr. Wahlberg declined to comment further on Saturday.

William Morris Endeavor said in a statement that it was "committed to being part of the solution." The agency pledged $500,000 to the Time's Up fund.

"The current conversation is a reminder that those of us in a position of influence have a responsibility to challenge inequities, including the gender wage gap," the statement said.

In a statement late Saturday, Ms. Williams gave credit to Mr. Wahlberg, William Morris Endeavor and many others for making the day "one of the most indelible" of her life.

"Today isn't about me," she said. "My fellow actresses stood by me and stood up for me, my activist friends taught me to use my voice, and the most powerful men in charge, they listened and they acted."

She continued: "If we truly envision an equal world, it takes equal effort and sacrifice."

Scenes from the movie, directed by Ridley Scott, had to be reshot after Imperative Entertainment, which financed the movie, removed the actor Kevin Spacey, who was accused by several men of making unwanted sexual advances, from the finished film.

Christopher Plummer replaced Mr. Spacey, and Mr. Scott reassembled the cast in London to reshoot the scenes with a budget of $10 million.

The film is about the 1973 kidnapping of John Paul Getty III and his grandfather's refusal to pay a $17 million ransom.

Fellow actors expressed outrage at the pay disparity when it came to light.

"She has been in the industry for 20 yrs," Jessica Chastain tweeted. "She deserves more than 1% of her male costar's salary."

On Saturday, actors expressed their support for Mr. Wahlberg's decision. Mark Ruffalo tweeted that the donation was "classy."

Octavia Spencer also praised Mr. Wahlberg, calling the donation a "good thing to do."

Melissa Silverstein, the founder of Women and Hollywood, a group that fights for pay equity in Hollywood, tweeted: "The lesson here is that pressure for equal pay works."

Also on Saturday, the actress Rebecca Hall announced her intention to donate her earnings from an upcoming Woody Allen film to the Time's Up fund. She wrote in an Instagram post that she shot scenes for the movie the day after accusations against Harvey Weinstein first broke. She added that she would not work with Mr. Allen, who has been accused of sexual abuse by his adopted daughter, Dylan Farrow, in the future. (Mr. Allen has denied Ms. Farrow's claims.)

"After reading and re-reading Dylan Farrow's statements of a few days ago and going back and reading the older ones — I see, not only how complicated this matter is, but that my actions have made another woman feel silenced and dismissed," Ms. Hall wrote.

MATT STEVENS contributed reporting.

As Obama Spotlights Gender Gap in Wages, His Own Payroll Draws Scrutiny

BY MICHAEL D. SHEAR AND ANNIE LOWREY | APRIL 7, 2014

WASHINGTON — President Obama on Tuesday will call attention to what he has said is an "embarrassment" in America: the fact that women make, on average, only 77 cents for every dollar that a man earns.

But critics of the administration are eager to turn the tables and note that Mr. Obama's White House fares only slightly better. A study released in January showed that female White House staff members make on average 88 cents for every dollar a male staff member earns.

The dueling statistics reveal the political sensitivities around a set of gender-related issues that could be critical in the midterm elections this fall. Those include pay equity, family leave, preschool and child care.

Mr. Obama and his Democratic allies are trying to portray Republicans as insensitive to the concerns of women, in the hopes of capitalizing on the kind of lopsided female support that helped Mr. Obama win the White House in 2008 and 2012. On Tuesday, Mr. Obama is to sign an executive order barring federal contractors from penalizing employees who discuss their compensation.

This week, Democrats in the Senate are to begin considering the Paycheck Fairness Act, which would add new regulations on how private companies pay their employees. Democratic lawmakers are seeking to overcome an expected Republican filibuster of the bill, which faces stiff opposition in the Republican-controlled House.

"The more light you can shine on wages, the better," said Heidi Hartmann, the president of the Institute for Women's Policy Research. "Who knows how much stronger enforcement it will lead to. But I think the publicity — the fact that people will hear about it and know about it — will help."

Even as Mr. Obama seeks to make an issue of the gender gap in compensation across the country, however, his own hiring is facing some scrutiny. The recent study, by the conservative American Enterprise Institute, showed that the median annual salary for women in the White House last year was $65,000, while the median annual salary for men was $73,729. The study was based on White House salary data.

The pay in the White House most likely mirrors the situation across the federal government, Ms. Hartmann said. "Women still tend to have lower pay grades than men do, because the men, on average, have more years of experience."

Jay Carney, the president's press secretary, said the statistics for White House staff members reflect the fact that women fill more lower-level positions than men. But he said that women and men in the same positions at the White House are paid the same, and that many of the women hold senior positions.

DOUG MILLS/THE NEW YORK TIMES

Senator Barbara A. Mikulski of Maryland, center, at a news conference in Washington on the Paycheck Fairness Act, which would add new regulations on how companies pay employees.

"Men and women in equivalent roles here earn equivalent salaries," Mr. Carney said. "Some of the most senior positions in the White House are filled by women, including national security adviser, homeland security adviser, White House counsel, communications director, senior adviser, deputy chief of staff."

He said that the 88-cent statistic was misleading because it aggregates the salaries of White House staff members at all levels, including the lowest levels, where women outnumber men.

Brendan Buck, a spokesman for House Speaker John A. Boehner, said the 77-cent statistic that Mr. Obama has often cited was misleading for the same reason, because it aggregates salaries for the American workforce. "The wage gap is real, but the White House does itself a disservice — and embarrasses itself in the process — by grasping for misleading statistics that don't tell the whole story," Mr. Buck said.

Mr. Boehner has long opposed new rules on equal pay, saying they are unnecessary because existing laws already prohibit workplace discrimination.

Mr. Obama has come under sustained criticism for appointing more men than women to his administration, though the gender breakdown of the White House staff itself is about even.

A study by the Center for American Women and Politics at Rutgers University, for example, found that women make up 35 percent of the president's cabinet. Although that is one of the highest proportions ever, it is down from the 41 percent hiring level during the Clinton administration.

"For men who are president, they have to make a conscious decision that they want to bring new faces into the mix," said Debbie Walsh, the director of the Center for American Women and Politics. "It's natural. And when you're the president of the United States, you want to be sure you can trust the people around you, that you know them, and that you've had a long-term relationship with them."

Referring to Mr. Obama's senior adviser, Ms. Walsh added, "That's one of the reasons Valerie Jarrett is there."

Gender Pay Gap? Maybe Not in the Corner Office, a Study Shows

BY ANDREW ROSS SORKIN | APRIL 23, 2018

THE PAY GAP between men and women has rightly become an important topic of conversation in offices and boardrooms across the country. Despite the efforts of some companies to address the disparity, women last year earned 82 percent of what men earned, according to a Pew Research Center report. The subject was the focus of a "60 Minutes" segment on Sunday night.

Now comes a bit of news that may spark some more discussion: There may be no pay gap at all between male and female chief executives of publicly traded companies.

That's the stunning conclusion of a new study by two professors who looked at the compensation of corporate leaders at 2,282 companies from 1996 to 2014.

The findings are sure to be controversial — though they shouldn't be considered a sign that the gender pay gap has meaningfully improved more broadly. Nor is it a sign that there has been a rush of woman appointed to chief executive. (There hasn't been.)

But it is a counterintuitive data point that is likely to be thrown into the mix of a debate in executive suites and boardrooms everywhere.

The authors of the study, Sandra Mortal, from the University of Alabama, and Vishal K. Gupta of the University of Mississippi (along with a researcher, Xiaohu Guo), called it a "welcome finding in today's zeitgeist of gender equality."

That's not to say the conclusion will be viewed positively.

Last year, The Wall Street Journal wrote an article with the headline "Female CEOs Earn More Than Male Chief Executives." It argued that female chief executives were being paid more than their male counterparts, with a median compensation level of $13.8 million, compared with $11.6 million for men.

The information was accurate. But the article was immediately criticized, both for being based on far too small a sample (there were only 21 female executives, compared with 382 men) and for a conclusion suggestive of a trend that is not a reality for most women.

Fortune magazine wrote that "such stories suggest that America's biggest corner offices are a haven for gender equity — which does not appear to be the case."

The new study, however, appears to be exhaustive.

"We controlled for several possible confounding factors," the authors wrote in a post on the website of Harvard Law School's Forum on Corporate Governance and Financial Regulation. Those factors included the chief executives' tenure, characteristics of the firms (size, performance and risk), and the size and independence of the boards.

The authors added that their model accounted for the fact that compensation for chief executives and the number of women in the role had increased over time. "Our results reveal that there is no significant difference between male and female C.E.O. compensation," they said.

The study also "casts doubt on the veracity" of the previous studies showing that female chief executives were paid more. "The truth seems to be that, once relevant confounding factors are accounted for, male and female C.E.O.s earn similar compensation, which is what standard economic theory would suggest and most people would like to see happen in society," they said.

One of the most interesting theories about why women may have bridged the pay divide at the highest levels has been offered by previous studies and experts: that a premium has been applied because there is such a limited supply of women in the chief executive role. Some readers may find that an offensive idea on its face — that women in effect are being overpaid because of their scarcity — but it's one that has gained currency among some academics.

In an interview, Professor Mortal said she was surprised by the results of her own study. "I would have expected that women were paid less," she said.

"There still is discrimination against women in getting to the top," she added, but said she welcomed the news that women were well paid "once they actually are there."

The authors acknowledged that in some extreme situations, men are still paid more by a wide margin. For example, Fast Company pointed out that in 2016, the highest-paid male chief executive was Tom Rutledge of Charter Communications, whose compensation was valued at $98.5 million, far beyond what Meg Whitman earned ($35.6 million) as the head of Hewlett Packard Enterprise. But Professor Gupta said such examples were "outliers in statistical language."

"It is certainly possibly that in the outlier group there is a gender difference, but we didn't look at that," he added, saying he was focused on averages.

He speculated that the pay gap at the top may have narrowed because the chief executive role is so publicly prominent. "We think it is a visibility issue," he said. "It is highly visible to all the stakeholders."

That may be true, but it doesn't explain why more public companies don't have female chief executives. Professor Gupta said that "is not an easy question to answer."

Perhaps providing a contradictory view, a recent study of nonprofit organizations found that there were more female chief executives than male, but notably, the women were paid less — 21 percent less if managing a budget of more than $50 million, according to GuideStar, a research firm that focuses on nonprofits.

The new study looked only at public companies.

Joanne Lipman, author of "That's What She Said: What Men Need to Know (and Women Need to Tell Them) About Working Together," said that irrespective of the study's results, "female C.E.O.s face a host of obstacles that male C.E.O.s do not."

"Female C.E.O.s should receive hazard pay," she said.

Ms. Lipman cited a handful of statistics that show female chief executives are more likely to be blamed for poor performance than their male counterparts; that women are disproportionately hired as chief executives in times of crisis, creating what has been called a "glass cliff"; and that female business leaders are often targeted more by activist investors, a topic that this column first raised in 2015.

There is, of course, a lot more research to do. It would be interesting, for instance, to better understand how the pay of female chief executives leads, or doesn't, to higher pay for other female executives.

But for now, perhaps this can be considered a little bit of good news in a journey that is far from over.

CHAPTER 3

The Economics of the Pay Gap

The reasons behind the pay gap are varied, complicated and widely debated. The general consensus among economists and sociologists connects the pay gap to a combination of factors, including legal obstacles, enduring sexism and gender discrimination, and challenges brought on by motherhood. Regardless of the cause, the consequences are certain: the pay gap exists and seems likely to persist for years to come.

Another Reason Women May Be Paid Less Than Men

BY TARA SIEGEL BERNARD | JULY 30, 2012

THE FACT THAT women continue to earn less than men has been well documented. And while part of that pay gap can be explained away, there is still a significant piece that cannot.

But new research suggests that the wage gap may potentially be attributed, at least in some part, to the way women are perceived in the workplace: When managers know they can blame the company's financial woes for their pay decisions, they are likely to give women smaller raises than their male counterparts. And that's because women may be seen as being more readily appeased by such excuses than men.

The findings, which came from an experiment conducted with 184 male and female managers with real-world experience who participated in a simulation, found that managers who worked about 13.5

years, which was the average for managers participating in the study, gave male employees 71 percent of money available for raises while they only allocated 29 percent of the funds to female employees. The results were even more pronounced among more experienced managers. (The study, "Engendering Inequity? How Social Accounts Create versus Merely Explain Unfavorable Pay Outcomes for Women," was recently published in the journal Organization Science.)

"Whenever research reveals disparities between men's and women's pay, there is a common retort: The gap must be due to unobserved differences in men's and women's willingness or skill in negotiating pay," said Maura Belliveau, the study's author, an associate professor at LIU Post's College of Management. "Although some gender differences in negotiation exist, this study reveals a major disadvantage women incur that precedes any negotiation."

The study's participants acted as managers and had to determine an employee's raise. The managers were told that raise funds were limited because of financial difficulties that were not yet public. The only factor that differed among the employees was their gender; everything else — including their job, level of performance and amount of money available for raises — was identical.

When managers could not explain their decision, they gave equal raises to men and women. But when managers could provide an explanation, they paid women less than men — but they also paid these women less than women in another situation where they could not provide them with an explanation for the raise amount. Raises given to men, meanwhile, were the same regardless of whether they could provide a reason or not. The results were consistent for both male and female managers.

By giving 71 percent of available raise money to men, Professor Belliveau pointed out that "managers ensured that men did not need to negotiate to obtain a good raise.

"In contrast, managers' raise decisions put women who performed at the same level as men in a position where they would not only need to negotiate to obtain a reasonable raise, but they would have to do so from the starting point of a lowball amount," she added. "That's an extremely challenging task, even for a skilled negotiator."

Professor Belliveau also studied why women were given smaller raises when managers had a ready excuse to fall back on. And she said that since women are stereotyped as people who are more focused on "process," the managers assumed women would feel that they were treated fairly when given an explanation. "Having the opportunity to explain enables managers to think of themselves as treating women fairly from a process perspective," she said. "So, paradoxically, managers who give women less pay can think that they are treating women well."

But research shows that managers' perceptions about women aren't rooted in reality. Past research shows that both men and women value fair treatment equally, she said. But the current study found that managers' ideas about women's values "loom larger than the objective reality, she added.

Data did not show that managers thought women would be more likely to believe the excuse, be more reasonable about pay constrains, or be less concerned about the size of their raises.

All of this obviously puts women in a tough position, which is why Professor Belliveau said that "managers and human resource professionals need to closely monitor pay data in their organizations to ensure that the burden of low raises is not disproportionately placed on women."

This is especially important now, she said, since many employers can easily use the current economy as an excuse for tightening the company's purse strings.

The Motherhood Penalty
vs. the Fatherhood Bonus

BY CLAIRE CAIN MILLER | SEPT. 6, 2014

ONE OF THE WORST career moves a woman can make is to have children. Mothers are less likely to be hired for jobs, to be perceived as competent at work or to be paid as much as their male colleagues with the same qualifications.

For men, meanwhile, having a child is good for their careers. They are more likely to be hired than childless men, and tend to be paid more after they have children.

These differences persist even after controlling for factors like the hours people work, the types of jobs they choose and the salaries of their spouses. So the disparity is not because mothers actually become less productive employees and fathers work harder when they become parents — but because employers expect them to.

The data about the motherhood penalty and the fatherhood bonus present a clear-cut look at American culture's ambiguous feelings about gender and work. Even in the age of "Lean In," when women with children run Fortune 500 companies and head the Federal Reserve, traditional notions about fathers as breadwinners and mothers as caregivers remain deeply ingrained. Employers, it seems, have not yet caught up to the fact that women can be both mothers and valuable employees.

This bias is most extreme for the parents who can least afford it, according to new data from Michelle Budig, a sociology professor at the University of Massachusetts, Amherst, who has studied the parenthood pay gap for 15 years. High-income men get the biggest pay bump for having children, and low-income women pay the biggest price, she said in a paper published this month by Third Way, a research group that aims to advance moderate policy ideas. "Families with lower resources are bearing more of the economic costs of raising kids," she said in an interview.

Cultural assumptions aside, here is the reality: 71 percent of mothers with children at home work, according to the Bureau of Labor Statistics, and women are the sole or primary breadwinner in 40 percent of households with children, according to data from the Pew Research Center.

Yet much of the pay gap seems to arise from old-fashioned notions about parenthood. "Employers read fathers as more stable and committed to their work; they have a family to provide for, so they're less likely to be flaky," Ms. Budig said. "That is the opposite of how parenthood by women is interpreted by employers. The conventional story is they work less and they're more distractible when on the job."

Ms. Budig found that on average, men's earnings increased more than 6 percent when they had children (if they lived with them), while women's decreased 4 percent for each child they had. Her study was based on data from the National Longitudinal Survey of Youth from 1979 to 2006, which tracked people's labor market activities over time. Childless, unmarried women earn 96 cents for every dollar a man earns, while married mothers earn 76 cents, widening the gap.

The gap persisted even after Ms. Budig controlled for factors like experience, education, hours worked and spousal incomes. It's true that fathers sometimes work more after children, but that explains at most 16 percent of their bonus, she found. And some mothers cut back on hours or accept lower-paying jobs that are more family-friendly, but that explains only a quarter to a third of the motherhood penalty.

The majority of it, research suggests, is because of discrimination. "A lot of these effects really are very much due to a cultural bias against mothers," said Shelley J. Correll, a sociology professor at Stanford University and director of the school's Clayman Institute for Gender Research.

Ms. Correll co-wrote a study at Cornell in which the researchers sent fake résumés to hundreds of employers. They were identical, except on some there was a line about being a member of the parent-teacher association, suggesting that the applicant was a parent. Mothers were half as likely to be called back, while fathers were called back slightly more often than the men whose résumés did not mention parenthood. In a similar study done in a laboratory, Ms. Correll asked participants how much they would pay job applicants if they were employers. Mothers were offered on average $11,000 less than childless women and $13,000 less than fathers.

In her research, Ms. Correll found that employers rate fathers as the most desirable employees, followed by childless women, childless men and finally mothers. They also hold mothers to harsher performance standards and are less lenient when they are late.

There was one exception in Ms. Budig's study: Women in the top 10 percent of earners lost no income when they had children, and those in the top 5 percent received bonuses, similar to men. She speculated that in these rarefied jobs, employers see high-performing women as more similar to men, and that women might work more and negotiate for higher pay in order to afford household and child care help.

At the other end of the earnings spectrum, low-income women lost 6 percent in wages per child, two percentage points more than the average. For men, the largest bonuses went to white and Latino men who were highly educated and in professional jobs. The smallest pay bumps went to unmarried African-American men who had less education and had manual labor jobs. "The daddy bonus increases the earnings of men already privileged in the labor market," Ms. Budig wrote.

That low-income workers benefit the least or suffer the most economically from parenthood is perhaps not surprising. They are the least likely to have flexible schedules or benefits like paid parental leave. Low-wage women with children under 6, when offspring need the most in-person care, paid a wage penalty five times as great as that of higher-paid women with young children, Ms. Budig found.

The data could be boiled down to hardheaded career advice: Men should festoon their desks with baby photos and add PTA membership to their résumés, and women should do the opposite. But ultimately, the solution is a realization that in the 21st century, male and female employees are not so different from one another.

"The best hope we have for getting rid of these effects," Ms. Correll said, "is policy that very much conveys that people have the right to coordinate work and family."

In Ms. Budig's previous work, she has found that two policies shrink the motherhood penalty: publicly funded, high-quality child care for babies and toddlers, and moderate-length paid parental leave. For instance, in countries that promote more traditional gender roles, like Germany, where new mothers are expected to take more than a year off work, the motherhood penalty is very high. Countries like Sweden with more progressive policies, such as incentives for new fathers to also take leave, have a smaller pay gap.

In the United States, most people eventually have children. That is a reality that employers should understand — as is the fact that now, fathers, too, change diapers and pack lunches and mothers go to work.

'Williams,' the Princess and the Gender Pay Gap

OPINION | BY CHARLES M. BLOW | FEB. 5, 2014

ONE DAY when my twins, a boy and a girl, were about 7 years old, we were out running errands.

We left one store and headed for the car. I entered the driver's door, my son got in the front passenger door, but I noticed that I didn't hear a rear door open and close.

I looked around to see that my daughter was still outside the car — her arms crossed, one hand clutching a little green purse made of stiff paper — staring disapprovingly at the door.

I rolled down the back window and asked, "What are you doing?"

She responded, "I'm a princess, and princesses don't touch doorknobs."

Having no idea where she had gotten such a notion, I was equal parts amused and irritated by it. I said, "Get in the car, sweetheart." She repeated her refusal.

This was now a standoff.

So, I started to inch the car forward as if I was going to leave without her. She jumped in the car in a huff: "Why didn't you open that door for me, Williams?"

"Who is Williams?" I asked.

"You," she said. "On TV when people have servants they're always called Williams or something like that."

I had had enough. I turned in my seat and explained to her that, yes, I did call her my princess, and although I loved her dearly, I would not pamper her. I told her that her value and worth were not in what men would do for her, but in what she could do for herself. I told her that in our family, as in life, she would have to be self-sufficient and self-reliant, and that included deigning to touch doorknobs, or in this case, car door handles. And I told her that if she ever called me Williams again, she would be punished.

Williams disappeared into the ether.

Now my daughter is a high school junior, a great student who often makes the honor roll, and a championship fencer who is ranked No. 2 in the country in her age group and weapon. She wants to go to college and study to become a doctor.

She has blossomed into the self-assured, self-sufficient and self-reliant young woman I hoped she'd become, and she now rails against, and writes about, gender bias and gender stereotype. But she still likes to carry a nice purse. Some things never change.

When I think of my amazing young lady going off into a world where there is still a gender-pay gap, it makes me furious.

I don't see this as a women's issue, but a societal issue and a moral one. This is not an issue for men to observe from a distance, because we are integral parts of it. First, there is little distance to be had: We all have mothers, and many of us have sisters, wives or daughters. Second, lower pay for women is only apparent in its relation to higher pay for men. So men are woven through the fabric of this issue.

A 2011 census report found that in 2010 "the earnings of women who worked full time, year-round were 77 percent of that for men working full time, year-round."

Now, part of that gap can be accounted for by the differences between men and women in the number of hours worked and the occupations chosen — take that into account and the gap is smaller. But those things also have an inherent gender bias because the "choices" women make are often based on slow-evolving gender constructs about who should do the majority of child-rearing and home-making.

A 2012 study by the Institute for Women's Policy Research found that, while the pay gap varied by occupation, "Women's median earnings are lower than men's in nearly all occupations, whether they work in occupations predominantly done by women, occupations predominantly done by men, or occupations with a more even mix of men and women."

Another 2012 study, this one by the American Association of University Women, found that even when men and women attend the same colleges, the gap persists.

According to the study "Graduating to a Pay Gap":

"In 2009 — the most recent year for which data are available — women one year out of college who were working full times earned, on average, just 82 percent of what their male peers earned. After we control for hours, occupation, college major, employment sector, and other factors associated with pay, the pay gap shrinks but does not disappear."

The researchers posit two theories that might help explain the gap: gender discrimination and gender differences in the willingness to negotiate salary.

When looking at doctors specifically, a study last year that was published in the Journal of American Medical Association found that while the gender pay gap is shrinking in the overall population, in the medical arena it has persisted — or even widened.

And, also to be sure that they were comparing apples to apples, the study cites data that "suggest that female physicians currently earn less than male physicians even after adjustments for specialty, practice type, and hours worked."

Even differences in special types, the authors write, "may be due not only to preferences of female physicians but also unequal opportunities."

These kinds of disparities and inequities are unconscionable, and men must be more vocal about saying so.

Why should a Dr. Williams be expected to make more than my Dr. Sword-Fighting Princess?

Vigilant Eye on Gender Pay Gap

BY TARA SIEGEL BERNARD | NOV. 14, 2014

THE FIRST STEP is admitting you have a problem, but it's another thing to actually address it.

Take the gender wage gap, for example. Women continue to make less than men for the same work, but a growing number of companies are quietly acknowledging that resolving the issue will require more effort than they've put forth so far. That means enlisting special teams to analyze whether their women are paid on par with equivalent men, job by job, then devising plans to fill in any gaps.

A majority of large companies in North America say they have dedicated teams running these pay equity analyses, but only 46 percent of them think their approach is statistically robust. Even fewer say they have a formal process to fix any inequities, according to a recent

ROBERT NEUBECKER

report by Mercer, the consultant, which examined 164 (mostly large) companies in 28 countries, employing more than 680,000 women.

Employers need to keep several data points on their workers to run the sophisticated assessments needed to tease out gender bias, academics said, and the depth of employers' human resources systems vary. But several companies — from diaper purveyors to military contractors who have them in place — said these systems had also helped them begin to tackle another related challenge: Why are so few women at the top of the organizations (or even the top of the middle)?

Flexible work schedules and generous leave policies aren't enough to solve that issue, and, in fact, can hurt women who use them if they aren't managed properly, research has found. But employers who actively manage pay equity tend to have positive ripple effects, consultants said, including more women in their senior ranks.

"You used to run these analyses only when risk and compliance had a concern," said Pat Milligan, president of Mercer's North American region. "Now, you are seeing companies — technology, consumer products, health care — do it to stay competitive, and they are doing it as part of an integrated strategy."

For some employers, a big motivation for running pay analyses is still to avoid lawsuits. Federal contractors must have the information on hand for potential audits. And soon, as part of the Obama administration's efforts to close the pay gap, contractors with 100 or more employees may need to file annual equal pay reports with the federal government, detailing salaries across job categories.

"They are doing it proactively, but it is a proactive response to risk," said Brian Levine of Mercer's work force strategy and analytics group, who said more companies had become interested in the reporting over the last five years.

Gap, the retailer, made a big splash this year when it said it had "equal pay for equal work," after validating its own findings with an independent external review.

Kimberly-Clark, maker of Kotex and Huggies diapers, built an analytics team over the last few years, which includes regular pay equity reporting. But the team also identified points where women were hitting a glass ceiling — two rungs up from entry level, and just before being promoted to a director. Since then, they've shepherded more women to the upper ranks: Now, women hold about 30 percent of director-level jobs or higher, she said, up from 17 percent in 2010.

"They have a developmental plan and we try to make sure we stick to it," said Sue Dodsworth, the company's global diversity officer.

Raytheon, a military and aerospace contractor, has been running pay equity analyses for 14 years, and said it had absolute pay parity across genders, something it says the government has verified through audits. Keith Peden, senior vice president for human resources and security, said all senior managers had real-time comparison tools on their desktops when making pay decisions. "These tools that we use help shape the behavior," he said. The company has 63,000 employees.

But one woman who works in Raytheon's engineering department, who did not want to be identified because she feared reprisals, said she felt the performance rating system was opaque. In her unit, she said the male-dominated culture made it difficult for women to move ahead. Mr. Peden acknowledged that as a male-dominated industry, the company had to work twice as hard to recruit and retain female engineers.

The city of Boston, through its Women's Workforce Council created last year, may have one of the more interesting strategies, bringing together the public and private sectors. So far, the council has persuaded 54 employers in the area to sign its "compact." Employers agree to take steps to close the pay gap and share pay data by gender and race — anonymously, for now — so the council can track the city's progress, said Christina M. Knowles, the group's executive director. The companies — Raytheon, State Street, MassMutual, BJ's Wholesale among them — will report base salaries and bonuses by

Christina M. Knowles, the executive director of Boston's Women's Workforce Council, which has persuaded 54 employers in the area to sign its "compact" to take steps to close the pay gap and share data.

job category, in addition to job-related data that many larger companies must already report to the federal Equal Employment Opportunity Commission.

"There isn't a desire here to embarrass any organization or to get them into hot water," said Alison Quirk, chief human resources officer at State Street, and a council member. "It's more that we all know we need to focus on these gender issues, so let's get a framework to do that."

At State Street, Ms. Quirk said her own company analyzed pay equity annually, but her larger struggle was filling the highest-paying positions with women and members of minority groups. While 40 percent of all assistant vice presidents are women, only 30 percent of vice presidents are women.

Dr. Levine of Mercer said pay gaps generally ranged from 2 to 6 percent, in aggregate and after controlling for legitimate factors, though certain pockets within organizations had greater disparities.

Their analysis shows that the imbalance often traces back to women being hired at a lower salary than their male peers. Other times, the lower pay is tied to a leave of absence, or reduced work schedules.

Naturally, paying women and minorities what they're worth will cost employers more money. The amount varies, but often runs about 0.5 to 0.8 percent of total payroll, according to Dr. Levine, in addition to any budget for merit increases. But what looks like a rounding error for big companies can translate into hundreds of thousands, perhaps millions, of dollars for women over their careers.

Other factors contributing to pay inequity, academics have found, is that women are less inclined to ask for raises, and perhaps for valid reasons: When they do, they are perceived as less likable and may be penalized as a result. Then there's the motherhood penalty, while other researchers found that women are often paid less than men in similar jobs because women are less likely to work the longest hours or specific hours — and those who do get disproportionate increases in pay.

That was the problem at Ryan, a private global tax services firm in Dallas, which had gained a reputation for draconian work conditions. It reached a tipping point when a valued female consultant gave notice, explaining that she had to leave because she was ready to start a family — and that wasn't possible at Ryan.

Shortly thereafter, in 2008, the company radically overhauled how all employees approached work and allowed them to work from the bathtub as long as they delivered results. All of the metrics feed into a calculator that suggests raises, which a compensation review committee also checks.

"It has really turned out to be a leveler in many ways," said Delta Emerson, Ryan's president of global shared services, referring to the results-focused approach. "In the old days, people could get by with having good relationships or the hours they put in. If you worked a lot of hours, you were a hero."

But even well-intentioned fixes need to be carried out thoughtfully, otherwise companies risk reintroducing gender biases elsewhere.

Emilio Castilla, a professor at the M.I.T. Sloan School of Management, found that employers that view themselves as meritocracies, rewarding performance, may pay men more than equally qualified women.

"The paradox of these merit-based practices," he said, "is that if they are not introduced properly, they can introduce or contribute to the pay gap we see in markets today."

In a coming study in which he examined nearly 9,000 employees' career histories at a United States company over many years, Professor Castilla found that white men born in the United States were given higher pay increases than women and minorities with the same performance evaluation scores, working in the same job with the same managers.

But the gap was no longer significant after the company created a series of new procedures, including a compensation committee that monitored pay decisions with written reports, for instance, and more formalized merit reward systems that hold people accountable. Managers could also see how their decisions compared with others, over all, at other units.

Without thoughtful fixes, the pay gap is likely to become like a game of Whac-a-Mole, and rear its head elsewhere.

Women Still Earn a Lot Less Than Men

EDITORIAL | BY THE NEW YORK TIMES | APRIL 14, 2015

TUESDAY IS EQUAL PAY DAY, the day selected each year by the National Committee on Pay Equity, a coalition of women's, civil rights and labor groups, to draw attention to how much longer women must work to earn what men earned in the previous year. In 1963, when President John F. Kennedy signed the Equal Pay Act, a woman working full time year-round typically made 59 cents for every dollar paid to her male counterpart. By 2013, the latest year of available census data, it was 78 cents on the dollar. Another measure of the wage gap, computed by the Institute for Women's Policy Research, shows that, in 2014, the ratio of female-to-male weekly earnings was 82.5 percent.

While that seems like steady if painfully slow progress, closer inspection shows that progress in closing the gender pay gap has basically stalled over the past decade. The longer the gap persists, the less it can be explained away by factors other than discrimination.

For example, recent research by the Economic Policy Institute shows that men still outearn women at every rung of the income ladder. The higher up the ladder, the bigger the gap. In 2014, women in the 95th percentile of female earners made 79 percent of wages for men at the 95th percentile, while women in the lowest 10th percentile made 91 cents for each $1 earned by their male counterparts. At the high end, corporate norms are likely the biggest factor influencing pay scales, and, while policies differ from company to company, the result is that women are still paid much less than men. At the low end, the minimum wage is a big factor influencing pay scales, and, since that applies to everyone, there is less pay disparity at the bottom of the ladder. Yet, even at that, women in low-wage jobs are paid less than men in low-wage jobs.

The gender pay gap is also pronounced among college-educated workers. The higher the level of education, the bigger the gap. Men and women who have attended but did not graduate from college have the narrowest gap, with women making about 80 percent of what men made (or about $16 an hour on average for women versus $20 for men). Among those who have graduated from college, women's pay is about 78 percent of men's pay (or about $26 an hour on average for women; $33 for men) and among those with advanced degrees, women make about 74 percent of what men make (or about $33 an hour on average for women; $44 for men).

Men even make more than women in traditionally female occupations. Recent research led by the University of California, San Francisco, shows that male registered nurses outearn female registered nurses by an average of $5,100 per year across most specialties and positions — an earnings gap that has not improved over the past 30 years. Other research has shown that male schoolteachers tend to outearn female schoolteachers.

In 2010, 2012 and 2014, congressional Republicans blocked consideration of the Paycheck Fairness Act, a bill supported by President Obama that would have extended pay-equity rules that apply to federal contractors to the entire American work force, in addition to making needed updates to the Equal Pay Act. Obstructionism has only made the problem worse, and an even more pressing one for the presidential candidates to address.

Is Planned Parenthood's President Overpaid?

BY MARGOT SANGER-KATZ AND CLAIRE CAIN MILLER | SEPT. 30, 2015

IN A LONG congressional hearing on Tuesday, Cecile Richards, the president of Planned Parenthood, fielded questions about her pay.

Jason Chaffetz, a Republican representative from Utah, said, "Planned Parenthood is an organization with massive salaries." It was part of his broader critique of the organization, whose clinics primarily offer reproductive health services for women, a small percentage of which are abortions. "Ms. Richards makes nearly $600,000 a year," he said.

He wasn't off by much. She was paid $427,597 last year — $590,928 if you include retirement contributions, bonuses and pay from affiliated organizations.

But that line of questioning angered Carolyn B. Maloney, a Democrat from New York, who accused Mr. Chaffetz of "beating up on a woman, our witness, for making a good salary." She called his comments "totally inappropriate and discriminatory" at a hearing that was really about continuing government funding of the group.

We can't hope to settle whether questions about Ms. Richards's pay are sexist. But we can see whether her pay was excessive for the industry. And in doing so, we can explore another issue — the possible sexism of a gender gap apparent in her pay.

Ms. Richards does make a lot of money relative to the rest of the American work force. Her pay puts her in the top 1 percent of all earners in the United States. But her salary is actually on the low side when it is compared with executive pay at other large nonprofits. When compared with the pay for hospital executives running nonprofit health care organizations of similar budgets, it is actually well below the norm.

Planned Parenthood brought in about $1.3 billion in revenue last year, according to its annual report, making it larger than the vast majority of nonprofit organizations in the United States. Among non-profit hospitals, only about 200 had higher revenue. Chief executives at hospitals of that size typically earn between $1.2 million and $1.5 million, said Dr. Ashish Jha, a professor at the Harvard School of Public Health, who has studied hospital executive pay.

Ms. Richards's pay is similar to that of a chief executive of a hospital with revenue a little more than a tenth of Planned Parenthood's — about $151 million, according to Dr. Jha's analysis of data from GuideStar, an organization that analyzes nonprofits' annual tax filings.

Many advocates for eliminating funding for Planned Parenthood have argued that federally qualified community health centers, which also serve many patients insured using Medicaid, could care for Planned Parenthood's patients instead. The National Association of Community Health Centers, the umbrella organization for those providers, brought in $34 million in revenue last year, according to company filings, a small fraction of Planned Parenthood's revenue. Its chief executive, Thomas J. Van Coverden, earned $690,284 in salary, and $1,006,012 in total compensation last year.

For those who might question whether health care companies are the right comparison, we also compared Ms. Richards's pay to compensation for executives across the entire nonprofit sector. As Mr. Chaffetz pointed out in the hearing, Planned Parenthood does engage in activities, including various types of political advocacy, that a traditional hospital does not. In GuideStar's report on nonprofit pay, among the 3,335 organizations in its highest budget category — nonprofits bringing in more than $50 million — average compensation is $689,973, about 17 percent more than Ms. Richards earns in total compensation.

We also looked at whether female executives in the nonprofit sector are paid less than the men. For a number of reasons, over all, American women are paid somewhere around 80 cents for every dollar that men earn.

There does appear to be such a gender gap in nonprofit chief executive pay, according to a GuideStar analysis of 2013 nonprofit pay.

Women were paid between 6 percent and 23 percent less than men, depending on the size of the organization, with the gap larger at the biggest organizations, though women tended to get bigger raises. The pay gap has increased over the last decade at all but the smallest and largest nonprofits. As in the for-profit corporate world, women are less likely than men to be executives at the very largest organizations.

Linda C. Babcock, an economics professor at Carnegie Mellon University who studies gender and pay, says researchers speculate that the larger disparity among nonprofit executives is because of gender biases on the part of boards. Directors might assume they must compete with for-profit salaries for men who could find high-paying jobs elsewhere, she said, but assume women are willing to receive lower pay in the nonprofit sector because they are working for a cause.

The pay gap for top executives seems to be bigger in the nonprofit world than in corporate America, where top female executives earn less than men on average, but earn more after controlling for their age and experience. That's because they are generally promoted earlier in their careers. (It's unclear whether that's true among nonprofit executives, too.) When it comes to additional compensation like bonuses, however, women receive bigger pay penalties than men for a company's poor performance and smaller bonuses for strong performance.

As Women Take Over a Male-Dominated Field, the Pay Drops

BY CLAIRE CAIN MILLER | MARCH 18, 2016

WOMEN'S MEDIAN ANNUAL EARNINGS stubbornly remain about 20 percent below men's. Why is progress stalling?

It may come down to this troubling reality, new research suggests: Work done by women simply isn't valued as highly.

That sounds like a truism, but the academic work behind it helps explain the pay gap's persistence even as the factors long thought to cause it have disappeared. Women, for example, are now better educated than men, have nearly as much work experience and are equally likely to pursue many high-paying careers. No longer can the gap be dismissed with pat observations that women outnumber men in lower-paying jobs like teaching and social work.

A new study from researchers at Cornell University found that the difference between the occupations and industries in which men and women work has recently become the single largest cause of the gender pay gap, accounting for more than half of it. In fact, another study shows, when women enter fields in greater numbers, pay declines — for the very same jobs that more men were doing before.

Consider the discrepancies in jobs requiring similar education and responsibility, or similar skills, but divided by gender. The median earnings of information technology managers (mostly men) are 27 percent higher than human resources managers (mostly women), according to Bureau of Labor Statistics data. At the other end of the wage spectrum, janitors (usually men) earn 22 percent more than maids and housecleaners (usually women).

Once women start doing a job, "It just doesn't look like it's as important to the bottom line or requires as much skill," said Paula England, a sociology professor at New York University. "Gender bias sneaks into those decisions."

THOKA MAER

She is a co-author of one of the most comprehensive studies of the phenomenon, using United States census data from 1950 to 2000, when the share of women increased in many jobs. The study, which she conducted with Asaf Levanon, of the University of Haifa in Israel, and Paul Allison of the University of Pennsylvania, found that when women moved into occupations in large numbers, those jobs began paying less even after controlling for education, work experience, skills, race and geography.

And there was substantial evidence that employers placed a lower value on work done by women. "It's not that women are always picking lesser things in terms of skill and importance," Ms. England said. "It's just that the employers are deciding to pay it less."

A striking example is to be found in the field of recreation — working in parks or leading camps — which went from predominantly male to female from 1950 to 2000. Median hourly wages in this field declined 57 percentage points, accounting for the change in the value of the dollar, according to a complex formula used by Professor Levanon. The job of ticket agent also went from mainly male to female during this period, and wages dropped 43 percentage points.

The same thing happened when women in large numbers became designers (wages fell 34 percentage points), housekeepers (wages fell 21 percentage points) and biologists (wages fell 18 percentage points). The reverse was true when a job attracted more men. Computer programming, for instance, used to be a relatively menial role done by women. But when male programmers began to outnumber female ones, the job began paying more and gained prestige.

While the pay gap has been closing, it remains wide. Over all, in fields where men are the majority, the median pay is $962 a week — 21 percent higher than in occupations with a majority of women, according to another new study, published Friday by Third Way, a research group that aims to advance centrist policy ideas.

Today, differences in the type of work men and women do account for 51 percent of the pay gap, a larger portion than in 1980, according to definitive new research by Francine D. Blau and Lawrence M. Kahn, economists at Cornell.

Women have moved into historically male jobs much more in white-collar fields than in blue-collar ones. Yet the gender pay gap is largest in higher-paying white-collar jobs, Ms. Blau and Mr. Kahn found. One reason for this may be that these jobs demand longer and less flexible hours, and research has shown that workers are disproportionately penalized for wanting flexibility.

Of the 30 highest-paying jobs, including chief executive, architect and computer engineer, 26 are male-dominated, according to Labor Department data analyzed by Emily Liner, the author of the Third Way report. Of the 30 lowest-paying ones, including food server, housekeeper and child-care worker, 23 are female dominated.

Many differences that contributed to the pay gap have diminished or disappeared since the 1980s, of course. Women over all now obtain more education than men and have almost as much work experience. Women moved from clerical to managerial jobs and became slightly more likely than men to be union members. Both of these changes helped improve wage parity, Ms. Blau's and Mr. Kahn's research said.

Yes, women sometimes voluntarily choose lower-paying occupations because they are drawn to work that happens to pay less, like caregiving or nonprofit jobs, or because they want less demanding jobs because they have more family responsibilities outside of work. But many social scientists say there are other factors that are often hard to quantify, like gender bias and social pressure, that bring down wages for women's work.

Ms. England, in other research, has found that any occupation that involves caregiving, like nursing or preschool teaching, pays less, even after controlling for the disproportionate share of female workers.

After sifting through the data, Ms. Blau and Mr. Kahn concluded that pure discrimination may account for 38 percent of the gender pay gap. Discrimination could also indirectly cause an even larger portion of the pay gap, they said, for instance, by discouraging women from pursuing high-paying, male-dominated careers in the first place.

"Some of it undoubtedly does represent the preferences of women, either for particular job types or some flexibility, but there could be barriers to entry for women and these could be very subtle," Ms. Blau said. "It could be because the very culture and male dominance of the occupation acts as a deterrent."

For example, social factors may be inducing more women than men to choose lower-paying but geographically flexible jobs, she and Mr. Kahn found. Even though dual-career marriages are now the norm, couples are more likely to choose their location based on the man's job, since men earn more. This factor is both a response to and a cause of the gender pay gap.

Some explanations for the pay gap cut both ways. One intriguing issue is the gender difference in noncognitive skills. Men are often said to be more competitive and self-confident than women, and according to this logic, they might be more inclined to pursue highly competitive jobs.

But Ms. Blau warned that it is impossible to separate nature from nurture. And there is evidence that noncognitive skills, like collaboration and openness to compromise, are benefiting women in today's labor market. Occupations that require such skills have expanded much more than others since 1980, according to research by David J. Deming at Harvard University. And women seem to have taken more advantage of these job opportunities than men.

Still, even when women join men in the same fields, the pay gap remains. Men and women are paid differently not just when they do different jobs but also when they do the same work. Research by Claudia Goldin, a Harvard economist, has found that a pay gap persists within occupations. Female physicians, for instance, earn 71 percent of what male physicians earn, and lawyers earn 82 percent.

It happens across professions: This month, the union that represents Dow Jones journalists announced that its female members working full time at Dow Jones publications made 87 cents for every dollar earned by their full-time male colleagues.

Colleen Schwartz, a Dow Jones spokeswoman said, "We remain absolutely committed to fostering an inclusive work environment."

Certain policies have been found to help close the remaining occupational pay gap, including raising the minimum wage, since more women work at the lowest end of the pay scale. Paid family leave helps, too.

Another idea, Ms. Liner of Third Way said, is to give priority to people's talents and interests when choosing careers, even if it means going outside gender norms, for instance encouraging girls to be engineers and boys to be teachers. "There's nothing stopping men and women from switching roles and being a maid versus a janitor except for social constructs," she said.

The Gender Pay Gap Is Largely Because of Motherhood

BY CLAIRE CAIN MILLER | MAY 13, 2017

WHEN MEN AND WOMEN finish school and start working, they're paid pretty much equally. But a gender pay gap soon appears, and it grows significantly over the next two decades.

So what changes? The answer can be found by looking at when the pay gap widens most sharply. It's the late 20s to mid-30s, according to two new studies — in other words, when many women have children. Unmarried women without children continue to earn closer to what men do.

The big reason that having children, and even marrying in the first place, hurts women's pay relative to men's is that the division of labor at home is still unequal, even when both spouses work full time. That's especially true for college-educated women in high-earning occupations: Children are particularly damaging to their careers.

But even married women without children earn less, research shows, because women are more likely to give up job opportunities to either move or stay put for their husband's job. Married women might also take less intensive jobs in preparation for children, or employers might not give them more responsibility because they assume they'll have babies and take time off.

"One person focuses on career, and the other one does the lion's share of the work at home," said Sari Kerr, an economist at Wellesley College and an author of both papers. One will be published in the American Economic Review this month; the other was published this month as a working paper by the National Bureau of Economic Research. The other researchers were Claudia Goldin of Harvard, Claudia Olivetti of Boston College and Erling Barth of the Institute for Social Research in Oslo.

It is logical for couples to decide that the person who earns less, usually a woman, does more of the household chores and child care,

Ms. Kerr said. But it's also a reason women earn less in the first place. "That reinforces the pay gap in the labor market, and we're trapped in this self-reinforcing cycle," she said.

Some women work less once they have children, but many don't, and employers pay them less, too, seemingly because they assume they will be less committed, research shows.

Even when mothers cut back at work, they are not paid proportionately less. When their pay is calculated on an hourly basis, they are still paid less than men for the hours they work, Ms. Goldin has shown in previous work. Employers, especially for jobs that require a college degree, pay people disproportionately more for working long hours and disproportionately less for working flexibly.

To achieve greater pay equality, social scientists say — other than women avoiding marriage and children — changes would have to take place in workplaces and public policy that applied to both men and women. Examples could be companies putting less priority on long hours and face time, and the government providing subsidized child care and moderate-length parental leave.

According to the data, Ms. Kerr said, college-educated women make about 90 percent as much as men at age 25 and about 55 percent as much at age 45.

The new working paper, which covered the broadest group of people over time, found that between ages 25 and 45, the gender pay gap for college graduates, which starts close to zero, widens by 55 percentage points. For those without college degrees, it widens by 28 percentage points.

Much of that happens early in people's careers, during women's childbearing years. The American Economic Review paper, which examined people born around 1970, found that almost all of the pay gap for college graduates came from ages 26 to 33. The researchers used demographic data from the 2000 census and work history from 1995 to 2008 from the Census Bureau's Longitudinal Employer-Household Dynamics program, which covers private-sector companies. These two data sets have rarely been combined, which allowed the researchers to connect people's work histories with demographic data like age, education, marriage and childbirth.

The pay gap is larger for college graduates because their earnings are higher, and men dominate the highest-paying jobs. These jobs also place more value on long, inflexible hours.

People without college degrees start out with a slightly larger pay gap, but it is smaller throughout their careers. Part of the reason is that less educated men have fewer high-paying job options than they used to. "The pay gap is not because non-college-educated women do so well, but because non-college-educated men are not doing well," Ms. Kerr said.

Twenty-seven percent of the overall pay gap is from men being more likely to jump to higher-paying firms, the economists found. When married women leave jobs, they are less likely to get a big pay bump as a result. Previous research has found they are more likely to leave without another job lined up; they may move for their husband's job or take time off with children.

But the bulk of the pay gap — 73 percent, they found — is from women not getting raises and promotions at the rate of men within companies. Seniority and experience seem to pay off much more for men than for women.

"On every possible front, women are getting the short end of the stick," Ms. Kerr said. "Whether they're changing jobs or trying to stick with the current employer, the returns are always smaller."

The average college-educated man, for instance, improves his earnings by 77 percent from age 25 to 45, while similar women improve their earnings by only 31 percent. Men without college degrees increase their earnings much faster than similar women in the first decade of their careers, but by age 45, women catch up.

Even women who catch up, however, pay a long-term price. They've lost a significant amount of pay — in wages, raises and retirement savings — along the way.

What We Talk About When We Talk About Pay Inequity

BY VALERIYA SAFRONOVA | FEB. 3, 2018

EARLY IN HER CAREER, Jewelle Bickford, now a partner at Evercore Wealth Management, worked at a global bank in New York with a male colleague who was on his best behavior during the first half of the day, she said, but during and after lunch, his work ethic devolved. "When he came back, you would walk by his office, and he would have his head down," Ms. Bickford said. "And you knew he had had quite a few drinks."

At the end of the year, when bonuses were announced, a friend of Ms. Bickford's who worked in human resources told her how much that male colleague had received. "It was many multiples of what I made," Ms. Bickford said. "He stayed there. I left."

It was a Monday in late January, and Ms. Bickford was at a table with four other women in a semiprivate room at Kiki's, a Greek restaurant in the Chinatown neighborhood in Manhattan. They included Gayl Johnson, a director of administration in New York City's Department of Sanitation; Alix Keller, the director of product technology at Hello Alfred, a home concierge service; Melissa Robbins, a Philadelphia-based political strategist; and Kimberly Webster, formerly a lawyer at a New York firm.

The women were of different backgrounds, ages and professions, but they had one thing in common: All said they had experienced gender-based wage discrimination over the course of their careers.

Though the pay gap has long been in the public consciousness — on average, American women make 80 cents for every dollar men make — three recent incidents have brought renewed scrutiny to an issue many women in the workplace say they continue to confront on an almost daily basis.

Early last month, Debra Messing and Eva Longoria chastised E! on the Golden Globes red carpet for paying Catt Sadler, the former co-host of E! News, half of what her male colleague, Jason Kennedy, made. (Ms. Sadler left the network in December.) The next day, Carrie Grace, the former China editor of the BBC, resigned that position after salary figures released by the broadcaster showed a gap between male and female talent.

And, of course, there is the perhaps the most famous recent incident — the revelation that Michelle Williams was paid $80 a day for reshoots on "All the Money in the World" while her male co-star, Mark Wahlberg, was paid $1.5 million in total (he later donated it to charity, following an outcry) — that got many women in offices around the country swapping tales of when in their own careers they found out they were being paid less than their male counterparts and what they did (or did not do) about it.

"I never really complained about the pay discrepancy," Ms. Bickford, 76, said, pausing between bites of moussaka. "I was brought up in a culture where it was considered gauche."

Five women, including Alix Keller, center, recently gathered over dinner to discuss one thing they all have in common: the gender wage gap. She was joined by Gayl Johnson, left, and (clockwise) Melissa Robbins, Jewelle Bickford, and Kimberly Webster.

"I missed that class," said Ms. Johnson. (Age? "You can say '55 plus.'") Ms. Johnson, who was sitting diagonally across from Ms. Bickford, took a bite of her lamb chop. "I've been doing this job for over 20 years," Ms. Johnson said. "I started as a clerk and worked my way up. I've had five promotions. But my white male counterparts earn $25,000 to $30,000 more a year than I do."

Ms. Johnson is one of 1,000 women on whose behalf a local union filed a complaint with the Equal Employment Opportunity Commission in 2013, claiming that the city paid women and minorities substantially less than their white male colleagues. In 2015, the E.E.O.C. ruled in favor of the women and recommended that the city negotiate a payout. The suggested starting point was $246 million. Though the city and the union came to a broad agreement last April, the details are still being worked out.

To help the union build its case, Ms. Johnson spent years gathering information. And she was not shy about demanding her rights. Once, she said, she called a supervisor and asked why she was making less than a male counterpart. The answer, she said: "He has a family to support."

Ms. Johnson is a single mother of three. Her experience is one example of what's called the motherhood penalty, a term for the economic and career setbacks women experience when they have children. (Men's earnings went up by more than 6 percent when they had children, if they lived with them, and women's decreased 4 percent for each child they had, a study found. And research has shown that employers rate fathers as the most desirable employees.)

Ms. Keller, 35, is raising a 9-year-old son alone. "I've made about 40 percent less than a colleague that's maybe only a tiny level above me, someone I didn't report to," Ms. Keller said. "I've been in a situation where a male colleague was making 100 percent more. I almost died inside."

Next to Ms. Keller was Ms. Robbins. "The last campaign I was working on, I told my campaign manager, 'We're going to lose if we do this your way,'" said Ms. Robbins, who declined to provide her age.

"Sixty-five percent of my salary was cut. My leadership as a black woman meant nothing to them."

Ms. Robbins described another job in sales where she asked for a raise, from $14 an hour, after bringing in a major client. According to Ms. Robbins, the company's owner refused. After quitting, Ms. Robbins said, a man was hired to replace her. His salary? More than twice as much. "That was the most humiliating experience that I have ever had," she said.

Sitting across from Ms. Robbins was Ms. Webster, 36, who says she left the law firm she was working for in 2016 after she wrote a letter to the partners suggesting that they were acting out unconscious bias. "At least for one case, and it may have been for multiple cases, my time was being billed out at a lower rate than two of the three white, male paralegals," Ms. Webster said. "The very next business day, I got put on a performance improvement plan," she added. "They were putting the paperwork in motion to either justify firing me or getting me to leave."

Retaliatory practices toward employees who complain about discrimination are far from abnormal. The E.E.O.C. reported that 48.8 percent of the complaints filed by workers in 2017 contained an allegation of retaliation.

Toward the end of the evening, entrees were forgotten and talk turned to the current moment and the future. "I believe we're at a tipping point," Ms. Bickford said. "The computer has really helped us disseminate information, and I think men are on notice now." Ms. Bickford and her colleagues in the business world have formed the Paradigm for Parity, which provides a five-step plan for gender equality that they have persuaded dozens of corporate leaders to implement.

Ms. Robbins was recently one of the speakers at the Women's March in Philadelphia and is working to help elect more female leaders. And Ms. Johnson plans to stick around in city administration and in the union as long as she can. "We have to look out for the ones who follow behind us," Ms. Johnson said. "There are more battles to be fought. Everyone deserves a chance."

The 10-Year Baby Window That Is the Key to the Women's Pay Gap

BY CLAIRE CAIN MILLER | APRIL 9, 2018

Women who have their first child before 25 or after 35 eventually close the salary divide with their husbands. It's the years in between that are most problematic, research shows.

TODAY, MARRIED COUPLES in the United States are likely to have similar educational and career backgrounds. So while the typical husband still earns more than his wife, spouses have increasingly similar incomes. But that changes once their first child arrives.

Immediately after the first birth, the pay gap between spouses doubles, according to a recent study — entirely driven by a drop in the mother's pay. Men's wages keep rising. The same pattern shows up in a variety of research.

But the recent study reveals a twist. When women have their first child between age 25 and 35, their pay never recovers, relative to that of their husbands. Yet women who have their first baby either before 25 or after 35 — before their careers get started or once they're established — eventually close the pay gap with their husbands.

The years between 25 to 35 happen to be both the prime career-building years and the years when most women have children.

The study — a working paper published by the Census Bureau in November — is one of several recent papers that show that children account for much of the remaining gender pay gap. That gap has narrowed significantly over the past four decades, as women have gotten more education and entered male-dominated professions, but a divide remains.

Women who have babies late typically have different career paths from those who have them early. Those who first give birth in their late 30s tend to be more educated with higher-earning jobs, while those who have babies in their early 20s have less education and lower earnings.

Even in families in which both parents work full time, women spend almost double the time as men on child care and housework.

Low earners have a smaller pay gap in general, and people who have babies in their late 30s could have a smaller pay gap because they are less likely to have more than one child. But the fact that both groups of women recover their earnings, relative to their husbands, suggests there's also something about having children outside the prime career-building years that hurts women's pay less, no matter the occupation.

One explanation is that the modern economy requires time in the office and long, rigid hours across a variety of jobs — yet pay gaps are smallest when workers have some control over when and where work gets done. In high-earning jobs, hours have grown longer and people are expected to be available almost around the clock. In low-earning jobs, hours have become much less predictable, so it can be hard for working parents to arrange child care.

The issue, in general, comes down to time. Children require a lot of it, especially in the years before they start school, and mothers spend disproportionately more time than fathers on child care and related responsibilities. This seems to be particularly problematic for women building their careers, when they might have to work hardest and prove themselves most, and less so for women who have already established some seniority or who have not yet started careers.

Women are more likely to reduce their work hours, take time off, turn down a promotion or quit their jobs to care for family. Even in families in which both parents work full time, women spend almost double the time on housework and child care. And when women work fewer hours, they are paid disproportionately less and become less likely to get raises or promotions.

"This shows that the birth of a child is really when the gender earnings gap really grows," said Danielle H. Sandler, a senior economist at the Census Bureau and an author of the paper.

The study found that over all, women earn $12,600 less than men before children are born and $25,100 less afterward. It analyzed earnings for opposite-sex, married couples who had their first child between 1978 and 2011, using earnings records from the Social Security Administration and data from the Census Bureau's survey of income and program participation. It includes women who were working two years before their first child was born, no matter how their hours changed afterward.

The pay gap grows larger with each additional child. It does not begin to shrink until children are around 10. For most women, their pay never reaches that of their husbands.

One surprise about the recent round of research is that the findings have been so similar in the United States and family-friendly Scandinavia. The two have very different economies and family policies, yet in both places, women's pay plummets after they have children. Scandinavian nations have generous paid parental leave as part of federal policy, while the United States government offers none.

It might be because both types of policies — no paid leave and very long paid leave — lead women to stop working. Economists have found

How a Common Interview Question Fuels the Gender Pay Gap (and How to Stop It)

BY CLAIRE CAIN MILLER | MAY 1, 2018

AILEEN RIZO was training math teachers in the public schools in Fresno, Calif., when she discovered that her male colleagues with comparable jobs were being paid significantly more.

She was told there was a justifiable reason: Employees' pay was based on their salaries at previous jobs, and she had been paid less than they had earlier in their careers.

Ms. Rizo, who is now running for the California State Assembly, sued. In April, the United States Court of Appeals for the Ninth Circuit ruled in her favor, saying that prior salary could not be used to justify a wage gap between male and female employees.

MIN HEO

It's the latest sign that this has become the policy of choice for shrinking the gender pay gap. Several states, cities and companies have recently banned asking about salary history. They include Massachusetts, California, New York City and Chicago, as well as Amazon, Google and Starbucks.

Women continue to earn less than men, for a variety of reasons. Discrimination is one, research shows. Women are also likelier than men to work in lower-paying jobs like those in public service, caregiving and the nonprofit sector — and to take time off for children. Employers often base a starting salary on someone's previous earnings, so at each job, the gender pay gap continues, and it becomes seemingly impossible for women to catch up.

"Women are told they are not worth as much as men," Judge Stephen Reinhardt wrote in the Ninth Circuit's opinion, before he died last month. "Allowing prior salary to justify a wage differential perpetuates this message, entrenching in salary systems an obvious means of discrimination."

What if job applicants don't live in one of the places where asking about salary history is banned? Some experts recommend that they find ways to politely deflect, although refusing to answer an interview question can be risky. Workshops by the American Association of University Women suggest some strategies.

Applicants could turn the question back on the employer by asking for the position's salary range, or what the last person to do the job was paid. Applicants could say something like: "I want to learn more about the job first, in order to have a better sense of my salary expectations." Or they could provide context for why they're declining to share the information, by explaining that it contributes to the gender pay gap.

Salary history bans can also have a less expected effect: When employers don't rely on past pay as a proxy for how valuable someone is, they might consider a wider variety of candidates. A recent working paper was based on an experiment in an online job marketplace: Half of employers could see applicants' past pay and half could not.

The employers who could not see past pay viewed more applications, asked candidates more questions and invited more for interviews. The candidates they hired had, on average, lower past wages, and struck better deals when they negotiated.

The study was not representative of most hiring situations — the job marketplace was for short-term projects on which applicants bid — and the experiment was not assessing gender differences in pay. But it showed that employers over-rely on past salary as an indicator of productivity, and without that information, they try to learn about candidates in other ways, said Moshe Barach, a co-author of the paper and a researcher at Georgetown.

"It takes more effort on the part of the employer, but they get better outcomes because someone who might not have made it to Step 1 now gets a chance," he said. "Employers talk to a person and might find they're really smart and hire them."

Salary history bans are too new for researchers to have studied their effects extensively. But other research has found that people are overly influenced by an opening bid, something social scientists call anchoring bias. This means that if employers learn an applicant's previous salary and it's lower or higher than they were planning to offer, it's likely to influence their offer.

When other types of information have been hidden during job interviews, it has led employers to discriminate less. A study of symphony orchestra directors found that when people auditioned behind a curtain, more female musicians were hired.

But the strategy can backfire. Some research has found that ban-the-box policies, which prohibit employers from asking on job applications whether people have criminal records, resulted in fewer black and Hispanic men being interviewed or hired. One theory is that without the information, employers assumed they had criminal records.

The same thing could happen with salary history bans, critics of the new policies fear. Employers could offer women and other targets of discrimination less because they assume they were paid less. Or women with high salaries might volunteer that information in interviews, leading employers to think that anyone who didn't share her salary had a low one.

Some business leaders have objected to salary history bans. The salary information helps them avoid interviewing people who would cost too much, they say. It can also help them avoid overpaying people whom they could hire for less, and it's a way to find out how much previous employers thought applicants were worth. The Chamber of Commerce for Greater Philadelphia fought a salary ban passed in Philadelphia, and this week, a United States district judge ruled that employers could ask about prior salary — but could not set pay based on it.

But using prior salary as a shortcut in that way also perpetuates discrimination, said Linda Babcock, an economist at Carnegie Mellon who has studied gender differences in negotiation. "The new law could make employers more purposeful about deciding ahead of time what they believe the position is worth," she said.

The salary history bans might spur other changes, by making people more aware of the problem, said Kate Bahn, an economist who studies gender and the labor market at the Washington Center for Equitable Growth. Employers might change the way they determine salaries or the way they respond to women when they negotiate, for example.

"That's part of why it may be such a useful small tool," she said, "because a lot of it is just sexism, and policy can help drive cultural shifts against sexism."

CHAPTER 4

Solving the Pay Gap

Economists, labor activists and politicians can agree that a gender pay gap exists, but they are less unanimous on the question of how to resolve it. For individual workers, litigation remains the only course of action available to them. Individual states have considered proposals ranging from pay transparency to a salary history ban. Some advocates have called for a more robust paid parental leave. This chapter shows the debate and the science behind this array of solutions.

Possible Path to Closing Pay Gap

BY SENDHIL MULLAINATHAN | MAY 10, 2014

IT'S 2014, and women are still paid less than men. Does this suggest that a gender pay gap is an unfortunately permanent fixture? Will it still be with us in 50 years? I would predict yes. But by that point, it will be men who will be earning less than women.

My forecast is based on evidence from schools, where it has been easier to work toward a level playing field than in the workplace.

Academically, girls have not merely caught up with boys in performance: they have overtaken them. In a study issued last year, and using data from 2000 to 2009, the economists Nicole M. Fortin, Philip Oreopoulos and Shelley Phipps found that 20.7 percent of female high school seniors had an "A" grade-point average, versus 14.7 percent of boys. In 2012, more than 70 percent of high school valedictorians were girls.

The trend extends into college. One study of Florida public colleges, by the economists Dylan Conger and Mark C. Long and covering the

years 2002 to 2005, found that women had higher grade-point averages and were also more likely to stay in school. And the Harvard economists Claudia Goldin and Lawrence F. Katz also show in their book, "The Race Between Education and Technology," how times have changed. They report that by the age of 30, a man born in 1945 was roughly 50 percent more likely than a woman to have completed college — but that men born from 1960 to 1975 were less likely to complete college than women. For the group born in 1975, the gap was nearly 25 percent.

"Whenever educational opportunities are made available on a relatively equal basis for females," Mr. Katz told me, "they tend to excel in completion and grades with some field differences."

As opportunities equalize in the workplace, will we also see a reversal of the gender pay gap?

One reason to think it's possible arises from why boys underperform in school in the first place. The prime suspect for this underperformance is boys' shortage of what social scientists call noncognitive skills. They have trouble sitting still, focusing and exerting self-control. Brian A. Jacob, an economist at the University of Michigan, found in a study published in 2002 that boys' behavioral problems explain a substantial share of women's advantage in college enrollment. One paper drove home this point by showing that girls outperform boys on tests requiring preparation, but not on those measuring aptitude.

Employers demand these same noncognitive skills. Those that it takes to succeed in college — time management, writing ability, structuring tasks on your own, working in teams — are also needed in the modern workplace.

Despite my crisp prediction, there are two reasons to believe that the trend seen in schools may not translate to the workplace. First, some evidence points to other gender differences in psychology. Laboratory experiments — many by the economist Muriel Niederle of Stanford — show that men fare better in competitive environments, in part because they are more confident. (Yes, overconfidence can be a help in such environments.) Even when a man and a woman perform equally well in a task — say, solving math problems — men are more willing to enter competitions based on that task. Men also show less risk aversion.

These differences — competitiveness, overconfidence and risk-seeking — could conceivably have greater benefits in the workplace, at least in some jobs, than they do in school.

A second factor is that jobs and society are still structured for traditional gender roles. Family commitments and household responsibilities will not disappear. Closing or reversing the gender gap, as Ms. Goldin noted in her presidential address to the American Economic Association, "must involve alterations in the labor market, in particular changing how jobs are structured and remunerated to enhance temporal flexibility."

It will also require change in social norms and identities, as the economists Marianne Bertrand and Emir Kamenica, at the University of Chicago, and Jessica Pan, at the National University of Singapore, have shown. They have found that if a woman is likely to earn more than her husband, based on a statistical prediction model, she is less likely to work outside the home. And when she does work and earn more, the marriages are less happy and more likely to result in divorce.

For the gender gap to reverse, these norms — or, at least, women's responses to them — would have to change. Ms. Bertrand notes that in Asia, "where gender norms are particularly strong, successful women are opting out of traditional family structures to focus on work." Rates of marriage and fertility are particularly low for successful Asian women. Of course, this may not be the way we would like to see norms change.

Ultimately, no one can predict with certainty the future of the gender gap; there are simply too many uncontrollable variables. But, clearly, the current debate is missing something.

If the pay gap leads us to consider men to be more productive than women, the schooling gap should symmetrically lead us to consider the opposite. Perhaps it is women who are more productive. If women's choices — such as taking time off to rear children — make them less productive in the economy, does adolescent boys' behavior in school make them even less so, because they are missing the educational potential of their formative years?

Maybe we shouldn't be asking when women will catch up. Maybe they've already caught up, and we should instead ask whether society is holding them back.

SENDHIL MULLAINATHAN is a professor of economics at Harvard.

How to Attack the Gender Wage Gap? Speak Up

BY JESSICA BENNETT | DEC. 15, 2012

ANNIE HOULE, grandmother of seven, holds up a stack of pink dollar bills.

"How many of you know about the wage gap?" she asks a roomful of undergraduates, almost all of them women, at the College of Mount St. Vincent in the Bronx.

A few hands go up.

"Now, how many of you worry about being able to afford New York City when you graduate?"

The room laughs. That's a given.

Ms. Houle is the national director of a group called the WAGE Project, which aims to close the gender pay gap. She explains that her dollar bills represent the amounts that women will make relative to men, on average, once they enter the work force.

Line them up next to a real dollar, and the difference is stark: 77 cents for white women; 69 cents for black women. The final dollar — so small that it can fit in a coin purse, represents 57 cents, for Latina women. On a campus that is two-thirds women, many have heard these numbers before. Yet holding them up next to one another is sobering.

"I'm posting this to Facebook," one woman says.

One of three male students in the room is heading to the photocopier to make copies for his mother.

Another woman in the group sees a triple threat. "This is crazy," Dominique Remy, a senior studying communications, says, holding the pink cutouts in her hand. "What if I'm all of them? My mother is Latina. My father is Haitian. I'm a woman."

I've come to this workshop amazed that it exists — and wishing that there had been a version of it when I was in school.

I grew up in the Girl Power moment of the 1980s, outpacing my male peers in school and taking on extracurricular activities by the dozen. I soared through high school and was accepted to the college of my choice. And yet, when I landed in the workplace, it seemed that I'd had a particularly rosy view.

When I was hired as a reporter at Newsweek, I took the first salary number that was offered; I felt lucky to be getting a job at all.

But a few years in, by virtue of much office whispering and a few pointed questions, I realized that the men around me were making more than I was, and more than many of my female colleagues. Despite a landmark sex discrimination lawsuit filed against the magazine in 1970, which paved the way for women there and at other publications to become writers, we still had a long way to go, it turned out.

When I tried to figure out why my salary was comparatively lower, it occurred to me: couldn't I have simply asked for more? The problem was that I was terrified at the prospect. When I finally mustered up the nerve, I made my pitch clumsily, my voice shaking and my face beet red. I brought along a printed list of my accomplishments, yet I couldn't help but feel boastful saying them out loud. While waiting to hear whether I would get the raise (I did), I agonized over whether I should have asked at all.

This fear of asking is a problem for many women: we are great advocates for others, but paralyzed when it comes to doing it for ourselves.

Back at the Bronx workshop, Ms. Houle flips on a projector and introduces Tina and Ted, two fictional graduates whose profiles match what's typical of the latest data. Tina and Ted graduated from the same university, with the same degree. They work the same number of hours, in the same type of job. And yet, as they start their first jobs, Ted is making $4,000 more than Tina. In the second year, the difference has added up to almost $9,500. Why?

"Maybe he just talked up his work more," one woman, a marketing major, suggests.

"Maybe he was mentored by other men," another says.

"Or maybe," chimes in a third, a nursing student, "she didn't know that she could negotiate."

Bingo. Over the next three hours, these women are going to learn how to do it — and to do it well.

There has clearly been much progress since President John F. Kennedy signed the Equal Pay Act in 1963, mandating that men and women be paid equally for equal work. Yet nearly 50 years later, if you look at the data, progress toward that goal has stalled.

Of course, not all statistics are created equal. Some account for education and life choices like childbearing; some don't. But if you sift through the data, the reality is still clear: the gender gap persists — and it persists for young, ambitious, childless women, too.

In October, the American Association of University Women — co-sponsor of the Mount St. Vincent program — offered a report called "Graduating to a Pay Gap," in which it determined that in their first year out of college, women working full time earned just 82 percent of what their male peers did, on average. Again, women's choices — college major, occupation, hours at work — could account for some of this. Even so, the A.A.U.W. determined that one-third of the gap remained unexplained.

For years, legislators and women's advocates have been seeking solutions. In many ways, the wage gap is a complicated problem tied to culture, tradition and politics. But one part of it can be traced to a simple fact: many women just don't negotiate, or are penalized if they do. In fact, they are one-quarter as likely as men to do so, according to statistics from Carnegie Mellon University. So rather than wax academic about the issue, couldn't we simply teach women some negotiation skills?

Ms. Houle, along with Evelyn Murphy, the WAGE Project president and a former Massachusetts lieutenant governor, aims to do just that. For almost seven years, Ms. Houle has been training facilitators around the country and introducing their program into schools. (WAGE stands for "women aim to get even.")

Now, working in conjunction with the A.A.U.W., they plan to have negotiation workshops — called Start Smart — in place by spring in more than 300 colleges and universities nationwide. Nearly 30 colleges have already signed up for three-year commitments.

Several other organizations have also begun working with schools, Girl Scout programs and Y.W.C.A.'s to coach women before they enter the work force.

At Smith College, the Center for Work and Life recently began a program called Leadership for Rebels that teaches young women assertive communication skills, through role-playing and workshops. At Carnegie Mellon, the Heinz School of Public Policy and Management will start its first Negotiation Academy for Women next month, led by the economist Linda Babcock. She is also the founder of a program called "Progress" that aims to teach similar skills to 7- to 12-year-old girls.

"I do think that people are really starting to take this idea seriously," says Professor Babcock, a co-author of "Women Don't Ask." "I think they're starting to understand that we have to train the next generation of women when they're young."

At Mount St. Vincent, the Draft 1 workshop is broken into sections: understanding the wage gap, learning one's worth on the market, and practical negotiation, in which students use role-playing in job-offer situations.

Women learn never to name a salary figure first, and to provide a range, not a number, if they're pressed about it. They are coached not to offer up a figure from their last job, unless explicitly asked. The use of terms like "initial offer" — it's not final! — is pounded into them. And, perhaps most important, they learn never, ever, to say yes to an offer immediately.

"I can't tell you how many times I hear stories of women who go into a negotiation saying, 'Oh my gosh, thank you so much, I'll take it!'" says Ms. Houle, noting that one student she coached even hugged her boss. "Here these women are, more educated than ever, incurring incredible debt to get that education, and they're going to take whatever they're offered. It's like, 'No, no, no!'"

Many reasons exist for women's fears about asking for higher pay.

There's the fear of being turned down. ("I think we take rejection personally," Ms. Murphy says.) There's the economy. (If you negotiate in a tough market, might the offer be rescinded?) There's the fact that women, in general, are less likely to take risks — a business asset in the long run, but one that can make advocating for themselves tricky. There's also the reality that many women have internalized the idea that asking is somehow not ladylike.

"Girls and women intuit that speaking up can be dangerous to your reputation — that asking for too much can be viewed as conceited or cocky," says Rachel Simmons, co-founder of the Girls Leadership Institute and a creator of the Leadership for Rebels program at Smith. "This may begin on the playground, but it extends all the way into the workplace."

Research by the Harvard senior lecturer Hanna Riley Bowles and others has found that women who negotiate are considered pushy and less likable — and, in some cases, less likely to be offered jobs as a result.

That's why women's approach to negotiation is crucial. In one study, from Professor Babcock at Carnegie Mellon, men and women asked for raises using identical scripts. People liked the men's style. But the women were branded as aggressive — unless they gave a smile while they asked, or appeared warm and friendly. In other words, they conformed to feminine stereotypes.

"The data shows that men are able to negotiate for themselves without facing any negative consequences, but when women negotiate, people often like them less and want to work with them less," says Sheryl Sandberg, Facebook's chief operating officer, whose forthcoming book "Lean In" is about women and leadership. "Even if women haven't studied this or seen this data, they often implicitly understand this, so they hold back."

So, it's a balancing act. Ask, but ask nicely. Demand, but with a smile. It's not fair — yet understanding these dynamics can be the key to overcoming them, Ms. Sandberg says.

The good news is that all of these things can be learned. In 2003, when Professor Babcock was conducting research for her book, she surveyed Carnegie Mellon graduates of the management school, determining that 13 percent of women had negotiated the salaries in the jobs they'd accepted, versus 52 percent of men. Four years later, after a lengthy book tour and talking relentlessly about these issues on campus, she found that the numbers had flipped: 68 percent of women negotiated, versus 65 percent of men.

Ms. Simmons put it this way: "This is about muscles that need to be developed. This is about practice."

And practice they will, one workshop at a time.

At the session at Mount St. Vincent, the women researched median wages and practiced speaking clearly and warmly. They tried to remember the three T's: tone (be positive but persuasive), tactics (never name a salary figure first) and tips (sell yourself, but anticipate objections; don't get too personal, but be personal enough).

"It was nerve-racking," said Ria Grant, a nursing student.

"I stuttered," recalled Danielle Heumegni, a sociology major.

And yet they felt good.

"I realized there's a way to sell myself without feeling uncomfortable," Dominique Remy said.

"You won't get anything if you don't at least try," said Erika Pichardo.

"This," Ms. Heumegni said, waving her set of pink dollar bills in the air, "was my aha! moment."

JESSICA BENNETT is the executive editor of Tumblr.

Let's Expose the Gender Pay Gap

OPINION | BY JOANNE LIPMAN | AUG. 13, 2015

HOW SERIOUS ARE WE, really, about tackling income equality?

The Securities and Exchange Commission took a shot at it last week, approving a rule that would require companies to disclose their C.E.O. pay gap — comparing how much chief executive officers take home compared with ordinary employees.

That's a fine idea. But here's a better one: require companies to publish their gender pay gap.

Think about it. Calling out top executives for making too much money will at most embarrass a few suits. But calling out companies for paying women too little will help millions — and perhaps crack one of the most intractable problems of our time.

More than a half-century after President John F. Kennedy signed the Equal Pay Act of 1963, the gap between what men and women earn

HANNAH K. LEE

has defied every effort to close it. And it can't be explained away as a statistical glitch, a function of women preferring lower-paying industries or choosing to take time off for kids.

Claudia Goldin, a labor economist at Harvard, has crunched the numbers and found that the gap persists for identical jobs, even after controlling for hours, education, race and age. Female doctors and surgeons, for example, earn 71 percent of what their male colleagues make, while female financial specialists are paid just 66 percent as much as comparable men. Other researchers have calculated that women one year out of college earn 6.6 percent less than men after controlling for occupation and hours, and that female M.B.A. graduates earn on average $4,600 less than their male classmates for their first jobs.

It's not that men are intentionally discriminating against women — far from it. I've spent the past year interviewing male executives for a book about men and women in the workplace. A vast majority of them are fair-minded guys who want women to succeed. They're absolutely certain that they don't have a gender problem themselves; it must be some other guys who do. Yet they're leaders of companies that pay men more than women for the same jobs.

Women are trying mightily to close that chasm on their own. Linda Babcock, an economist at Carnegie Mellon and co-author of the book "Women Don't Ask," has found that one reason for the disparity is that men are four times more likely to ask for a raise than women are, and that when women do ask, we ask for 30 percent less. And so women are told we need to lean in, to demand to be paid what we're worth. It's excellent advice — except it isn't enough.

There is an antidote to the problem. Britain recently introduced a plan requiring companies with 250 employees or more to publicly report their own gender pay gap. It joins a handful of other countries, including Austria and Belgium, that have introduced similar rules. (In the United States, President Obama last year signed a presidential memorandum instructing federal contractors to report wage information by gender and race to the Department of Labor.) The disclosures "will cast sunlight on the discrepancies and create the pressure we need for change, driving women's wages up," Prime Minister David Cameron said last month.

Critics of the British plan protest that it's too expensive and complex. Some contend that it doesn't address the root of the problem: systemic issues that block women from higher-paying industries, and social issues like unconscious bias.

But real-world results suggest otherwise. Last year, the consulting firm PricewaterhouseCoopers voluntarily released its gender pay gap in Britain, one of five firms in the country, including AstraZeneca, to do so. Simply saying the number out loud "created much more momentum internally" to close it, Sarah Churchman, who runs the firm's British diversity and inclusion efforts, told me.

PricewaterhouseCoopers's analysis showed that most of its 15.1 percent pay disparity (compared with a Britain-wide gap of more than 19 percent) reflected a lack of women in senior jobs. So the firm focused on whether it was promoting fairly. In 2013, the grade just below partner was 30 percent female, yet only 16 percent of those promoted to partner were women. A year later, the percentage of women promoted to partner had more than doubled.

The firm's executives were also stunned to find a bonus pattern that favored men. The analysis showed that men who were passed over for partnership were routinely offered retention bonuses to keep them from quitting. Women weren't. Ms. Churchman believes that's because men often threatened to leave, while women typically decided to work harder and try again next year.

The potential cost savings of publishing the gender wage gap are enormous. About 20 percent of large companies now train employees to recognize unconscious bias, spending billions of dollars to try to stamp out unintentional discrimination. Paying for a salary analysis is cheaper and potentially more effective. Evidence also suggests that less secrecy about pay results in greater employee loyalty and lower turnover.

There's a strong argument to be made for transparency not just for women, but for minorities and other disadvantaged groups. African-American men earn less than white men, for example, though a Harvard Business Review analysis found that controlling for education, black men out-earn both white and black women.

Political realities being what they are, the chances of achieving that kind of transparency are slim; even the tepid C.E.O. pay gap rule took the S.E.C. five years to push through, in the face of fierce industry opposition.

But why would we not want a measure that will settle the controversy over the pay gap with quantifiable facts? Shining some much-needed sunlight on the gender wage gap will make a difference for every one of us, men and women, right now.

JOANNE LIPMAN is working on a book about men and women at work. She is a former editor at The Wall Street Journal and editor of Conde Nast Portfolio.

How to Bridge That Stubborn Pay Gap

BY CLAIRE CAIN MILLER | JAN. 15, 2016

WHEN THE COMEDIAN Ricky Gervais joked that he was paid the same to host the Golden Globes as the actresses Tina Fey and Amy Poehler — combined — his barbed humor most likely resonated in many workplaces.

More than a half-century after President John F. Kennedy signed the Equal Pay Act, the gender pay gap is still with us. Women earn 79 cents for every dollar men earn, according to the Census Bureau.

That statistic is based on the median salaries of full-time workers, not men and women doing the same jobs, but other data show that the gap occurs in a broad range of occupations. Women who are surgeons earn 71 percent of what men earn, while food preparers earn 87 percent, according to data from Claudia Goldin, a Harvard economist.

The gap cannot be entirely explained by anything economists can measure — workers' education and experience, the jobs they choose, the hours they work or the time they take off. That leaves other factors that are hard to quantify, like discrimination or women's perception of the choices available to them.

So what might work to close the gap? Social scientists and policy makers have some ideas, as do companies that have been trying to combat the problem in their work forces.

PUBLISH EVERYONE'S PAY

When employers publish people's salaries, the pay gap shrinks.

Jake Rosenfeld, a sociologist at Washington University, has found that salary transparency raises wages, in part by lending legitimacy to employees' arguments in wage bargaining. "Even being cognizant of gender pay disparity being an issue can change norms," he said.

That has been true in the public sector, where disclosing pay information is often required. Alexandre Mas, an economist at Princeton, studied the effects of a 2010 California law that required cities to publish municipal salaries. It prompted pay cuts, but only among men.

Women might have been spurred to negotiate after seeing that their salaries were lower, he theorized, or cities might have made salaries more equitable to avoid lawsuits.

A few European countries have required that big companies publish pay information by sex. President Obama in 2014 required that federal contractors report it to the Labor Department. Other American companies say they have analyzed pay this way, though most do it privately.

Marc Benioff, the C.E.O of Salesforce.com, said last year that after such an analysis, the company spent $3 million to make women's salaries equal to men's. Kimberly-Clark and PricewaterhouseCoopers have said their examinations led managers to address the fact that fewer women were reaching top positions.

TO NEGOTIATE, OR NOT

Men are paid more partly because they're much more likely to ask for it.

When receiving job offers, 51.5 percent of men and 12.5 percent of women asked for more money, according to a study of Carnegie Mellon University graduate students by Linda Babcock, an economist at the university. In other research, she found that when women did ask, they asked for 30 percent less than men requested.

Because starting salaries determine raises and future salaries, women who do not bargain lose as much as $750,000 for middle-income jobs and $2 million for high-income jobs over their careers, Ms. Babcock found.

But her research and that of others has found that women are penalized for negotiating, while men are rewarded for the same behavior. (As the actress Jennifer Lawrence wrote in Lenny after the Sony hacking revealed that she was paid less than her male co-stars, she didn't fight for more because "I didn't want to seem 'difficult' or 'spoiled.' ")

One solution, Ms. Babcock said, is to coach women to negotiate. Another is to change corporate practices so the people who set compensation are aware of the disparity and are advocates for women during negotiations.

Another answer is to ban pay negotiation completely. That is what Ellen Pao did when she was chief executive of Reddit. The company established pay ranges based on roles and experience and gave applicants nonnegotiable offers.

"We put the onus on the company to pay fairly instead of on candidates to negotiate fair pay," Ms. Pao wrote in The Hollywood Reporter.

DON'T RELY ON PREVIOUS SALARIES

If women can lose millions over their careers because they get job offers based on pay that is already low, one way to stop the pattern is to ignore their past salaries.

Google has said it does this and instead makes offers based on what a job is worth.

In August, the federal Office of Personnel Management said government hiring managers could no longer rely on an employee's previous salary when setting his or her new one. The acting director, Beth Cobert, explained that the practice particularly disadvantaged women who had taken time off to raise children. Women are also more likely to have worked in the lower-paying public or nonprofit sectors.

"Don't ask about salary history for new hires, and it really reduces the impact of previous discrimination," Ms. Babcock said. "I think that is the most effective thing organizations can do."

MAKE WORK EASIER FOR MOTHERS

Research has found that salaries at men and women's first jobs out of school are fairly similar. The gender pay gap widens a few years later when women start having children.

Sometimes their pay lags because they take breaks from work when their children are young, work fewer hours or take more time off than men for child care crises. Sometimes their employers assume they'll do so, even if they don't.

Policies that help keep women in the work force, like affordable child care, paid sick days and parental leave, could help. In states that offer paid parental leave, for instance, mothers are more likely to return to work, work more hours and earn higher wages, economists have found.

"If a cashier gets pregnant, has no parental leave, has to leave and reapply for her job, that's not the same as making a career choice," said Philip Cohen, a sociologist at the University of Maryland. "One thing policy can do is make it easier for women to stick with their careers."

BUILD MORE FLEXIBLE WORKPLACES

Ms. Goldin of Harvard has found that the pay gap is largest in occupations with the least flexibility in terms of where and when people work, like finance and medicine. The gap shrinks when people can work on their own schedules, as in many tech jobs and when people can easily substitute for one another, as happens among pharmacists. Then, women aren't penalized as much for working fewer hours.

Companies might address the culture of face time and overwork, and change how they operate. In a pharmacy, for instance, electronic medical records have made it easier for different pharmacists to serve the same patient.

CHANGE THE LAW

Federal law doesn't require most of these things, so some lawmakers are trying other tactics.

The strongest equal pay bill in the country went into effect in California this month. It says that men and women must be paid the same for similar jobs, not just for exactly the same job at the same site, as the looser federal Equal Pay Act requires. The California law also prohibits employers from retaliating against workers for discussing pay.

Proposed federal legislation known as the Paycheck Fairness Act would require companies to report pay data to the government, give grants for negotiation training and make class-action lawsuits easier. But that legislation is stalled in Congress.

Illegal in Massachusetts: Asking Your Salary in a Job Interview

BY STACY COWLEY | AUG. 2, 2016

IN A GROUNDBREAKING EFFORT to close the wage gap between men and women, Massachusetts has become the first state to bar employers from asking about applicants' salaries before offering them a job.

The new law will require hiring managers to state a compensation figure upfront — based on what an applicant's worth is to the company, rather than on what he or she made in a previous position.

The bipartisan legislation, signed into law on Monday by Gov. Charlie Baker, a Republican, is being pushed as a model for other states, as the issue of men historically outearning women who do the same job has leapt onto the national political scene.

Nationally, there have been repeated efforts to strengthen equal pay laws — which are already on the books but tend to lack teeth — but none have succeeded so far. Hillary Clinton has tried to make equal pay a signature issue of her campaign, while Donald J. Trump's daughter Ivanka praised her father for his actions on this issue when she spoke at the Republican National Convention.

By barring companies from asking prospective employees how much they earned at their last jobs, Massachusetts will ensure that the historically lower wages and salaries assigned to women and minorities do not follow them for their entire careers. Companies tend to set salaries for new hires using their previous pay as a base line.

"I think very few businesses consciously discriminate, but they need to become aware of it," said State Senator Pat Jehlen, a Democrat and one of the bill's co-sponsors. "These are things that don't just affect one job; it keeps women's wages down over their entire lifetime."

Federal law already prohibits gender-based pay discrimination, but violations are hard to prove and wage gaps persist in nearly every industry.

Nationally, women are paid 79 cents for every dollar that men earn, according to the United States Census Bureau. A number of factors affect that statistic, including the career fields women choose, but economists consistently find evidence of pay disparities not offset by other variables.

The Massachusetts law, which will go into effect in July 2018, takes other steps as well to combat pay discrimination. Companies will not be allowed to prohibit workers from telling others how much they are paid, a move that proponents say can increase salary transparency and help employees discover disparities.

And the law will require equal pay not just for workers whose jobs are alike, but also for those whose work is of "comparable character" or who work in "comparable operations." Workers with more seniority will still be permitted to earn higher pay, but the law effectively broadens the definition of what is equal work.

Other states have also been stepping up their protections. In May, Maryland passed a law that requires equal pay for "comparable" work, and California last year enacted a law that is one of the nation's strictest, requiring employers to be able to prove that they pay workers of both genders equally for "substantially similar" jobs. It, too, had the backing of important local trade groups, including the California Chamber of Commerce.

And Massachusetts joins at least 12 other states that already require companies to let employees compare notes about how much they are paid.

The distinguishing feature in the Massachusetts law is that job seekers will no longer be compelled to disclose their salary or wages at their current or previous jobs — which often leaves applicants with the nagging suspicion that they might have been offered more money if the earlier figure had been higher. People will still be allowed to volunteer their salary information.

"This is a sea change, and we hope it will be used as a model in other states," said Victoria A. Budson, executive director of the

Women and Public Policy Program at Harvard's Kennedy School of Government and chairwoman of the Massachusetts Commission on the Status of Women. The law in her state, she said, "will help every single individual who applies for a job, not just women."

Efforts to pass a national anti-secrecy law, the Paycheck Fairness Act, have been repeatedly blocked by congressional Republicans. Opponents, including the U.S. Chamber of Commerce, a powerful business lobbying group, say that such laws would increase litigation and unfairly restrict employers' compensation decisions.

But proponents of equal pay laws say that attitudes are shifting among businesses. In Massachusetts, for instance, the Greater Boston Chamber of Commerce was an early and enthusiastic backer.

"That really set the tone," said State Representative Ellen Story, a Democrat and co-sponsor of the bill. "Now it wasn't just members of the women's caucus, it was business leaders, too, asking for this."

The Massachusetts attorney general will be in charge of enforcing the law, which also gives workers the right to sue companies directly for violations.

In June, 28 businesses nationwide, including large employers like Gap, Pepsi and American Airlines, signed an Equal Pay Pledge promoted by the White House in which they committed to conducting annual audits of their pay by gender across all job categories.

"Companies that want to do the right thing are seeing that these new laws really pose no threat," said Vicki Shabo, vice president of the National Partnership for Women & Families, which tracks the fair pay bills introduced in state legislatures. "It's absolutely started to pick up. These laws are not just passing in completely blue places," she added, "they're passing with bipartisan votes."

Businesses are also beginning to talk more openly about the often uncomfortable things those audits find. PricewaterhouseCoopers published the results of a pay analysis it did of its British staff. It found a 15.1 percent pay disparity between men and women, and changed its promotion practices to bring more women into senior leadership roles. Salesforce, a cloud software company, says it spent $3 million last year to raise the salaries of female employees to match their male counterparts.

Academic research has illustrated the negative effect pay disparity has not just on individuals, but also on the broader economy. Closing the gender wage gap would lower the poverty rates in every state, according to an analysis by the Institute for Women's Policy Research.

Just as important, according to advocates of equal pay, are the changing demographics in boardrooms and statehouses.

Ms. Jehlen, one of the Massachusetts bill's co-sponsors, recalled the first time she testified about equal pay issues before the legislature's labor committee: All the members were men.

She and others had taken up the cause on behalf of a group of female cafeteria workers who filed a lawsuit in 1991 seeking parity with male janitors, who did comparable work, the cafeteria workers said, but were paid significantly more. The Massachusetts Supreme Judicial Court ruled against the women, saying that the state's equal pay law was not clear in its definition of comparable work.

This week, one of those cafeteria workers attended the ceremony at which Governor Baker signed the new law.

"For me," Ms. Jehlen said, "that was the most emotionally powerful thing."

Room for Debate: How to Reduce the Pay Gap Between Men and Women

OPINION | BY THE NEW YORK TIMES | AUG. 15, 2016

MASSACHUSETTS NOW MANDATES that employers offer prospective employees a compensation figure without asking what that applicant made at a previous job, to keep from perpetuating the disparately low wages that plague women and minorities. New York City is considering a similar bill.

But the causes of pay inequity are complex. Are these measures a step in the right direction? What else can be done to ensure women receive equal pay for equal work?

WOMEN NEED EQUAL OPPORTUNITIES FOR JOB ADVANCEMENT

HEIDI HARTMANN, an economist, is the president and founder of the Institute for Women's Policy Research.

The new Act to Establish Pay Equity in Massachusetts is similar to voluntary moves by Google and other companies that have changed their hiring policies to base a salary offer on the market rate of the job, not on previous compensation.

The Massachusetts law also improves pay transparency by forbidding employers from discouraging workers to compare notes on their salaries.

Both of these requirements should help equalize pay for women and men doing similar work, but while this effort is both needed and welcome, don't expect it to end the gender wage gap on its own.

Across the economy, despite decades of female progress in entering higher-paying jobs formerly done almost exclusively by men, about 40 percent of women and 50 percent of men still work in occupations that are dominated by their own gender. Typically, in smaller segments of the economy — such as within a single firm or field — sex segregation among occupations is even greater. Different entry level jobs go disproportionately to men and women. For example, a Home Depot in Southern California settled with the Office of Federal Contract Compliance in 2015, including a back pay award, because it had typically assigned women to roles as cashiers and men to roles as sales associates — a higher paying job with more upward mobility.

More broadly, it is too often forgotten that hiring managers can choose where new entrants are assigned. While Title VII of the 1964 Civil Rights Act is designed to prevent such stereotypical hiring, much of it remains. When examining pay distribution in their businesses, employers should look beyond equal pay for similar work, to whether women have equal opportunity to work in the highest paid jobs and are able to advance up the ranks.

SALARY TRANSPARENCY IS KEY TO NARROWING GENDER PAY DISPARITIES

JAKE ROSENFELD, an associate professor of Sociology at Washington University-St. Louis, is the author of "What Unions No Longer Do."

Similar to a provision in the Massachusetts new law, California recently passed legislation that prohibits employers from penalizing workers who discuss wages and salaries. (Massachusetts goes further by also restricting employers from asking about new hires' salary histories.)

These laws are useful in helping to erode the norm against discussing wages and salaries. Sapping the strength of this longstanding cultural prohibition could empower women and racial and ethnic minority workers to speak out against unfair pay practices, and potentially reduce stubborn pay gaps.

I say potentially because the actual impact of these laws will depend on their enforcement, and just as important, on education campaigns to let workers know these laws are on the books. After all, policies that prohibit workers from discussing their pay with colleagues have been illegal for over 80 years. And yet we know from a recent survey that nearly half of the workforce remains subject to this type of speech restriction.

Similarly, banning the use of salary histories in setting pay will matter only if workers and hiring managers are aware of Massachusetts' new law.

And, like other recent legislation, Massachusetts's does not mandate salary transparency — which could be a big step toward eliminating the pay gap. It aims only to prevent employers from penalizing workers who discuss wages and salaries. There is a huge gulf between pay transparency — like we see in many public sector settings, where wage gaps between men and women tend to be lower — and these recent policies to help narrow gender pay disparities.

After all, allowing workers to discuss pay will reduce disparities only if underpaid workers actually have these conversations, and then demand a raise, and their bosses meet their demands.

SALARY NEGOTIATIONS OFTEN PRECLUDE WOMEN FROM EQUAL PAY

NICOLE PORTER is a law professor at the University of Toledo.

Most of the pay gap between men and women is not caused by intentional discrimination by employers. But that doesn't mean that discrimination doesn't exist.

Employers often rely on what I have called "market excuses." One of those market excuses is when employers rely on what an applicant was making in a prior job in order to set that applicant's pay. Because women have historically been paid less than men (for reasons both lawful and unlawful), that pay disparity perpetuates itself when employers base current salary on prior salary. So Massachusetts's new law is an important step in ending the reliance on this market excuse.

It will arguably force an employer to offer a salary based on what the position is worth to the company — not based on what an employee was previously earning.

The law also contains other helpful provisions: It prohibits employers from penalizing employees from talking about their wages; it uses the broader "comparable work" rather than "equal work" when establishing the similarity between two positions; and it doesn't give employers the catch-all defense contained in the Equal Pay Act — that a pay differential between men and women for equal work is not unlawful if it is based on "any other factor other than sex." This catch-all defense has allowed employers to rely on market excuses, such as prior salary, when setting pay. As a whole, I would be delighted if other states and the federal government adopted legislation similar to Massachusetts's new law.

But the legislation does not go far enough in one respect.

Because it forbids employers only from seeking prior salary information, it does not preclude applicants from voluntarily disclosing that information and then using it to negotiate a higher salary. A voluminous amount of literature makes clear that (as a general rule, subject to many exceptions) women do not negotiate on their own behalf as often as men. The reasons for this are numerous and complex, but simply stated, women have been socialized to believe asking on their own behalf is a gender norm violation.

Women's experience often bears out this belief, as many experience resentment or even withdrawn offers when they do try to negotiate for a better compensation package. As long as employers are allowed to pay unequal wages to men and women doing comparable work simply because the men negotiated for more (perhaps after voluntarily disclosing a higher prior salary) we will not completely eradicate the pay gap.

The bottom line is: The new law in Massachusetts is laudable and worthy of emulation but could go further to fully remedy the pay gap.

PROFESSIONS ASSOCIATED WITH WOMEN ARE LOWER PAID

AI-JEN POO is the director of the National Domestic Workers Alliance and co-director of the Caring Across Generations campaign.

Preventing employers from basing new salaries on previous ones could interrupt the lifelong trajectory of lower wages that begins early in women's careers. But there are larger patterns and manifestations of gender inequality in our economy that we must also disrupt.

The way we value work itself often has to do with gender and race: Work that is associated with women, particularly immigrant women and women of color, is less valued. Two thirds of all minimum wage workers today are women, and many minimum wage jobs have highly disproportionate concentrations of women of color. Care jobs are the quintessential example: At a median annual wage of $13,000, those who work in our homes as home care workers are barely able to care for their own families on their earnings.

One housecleaner I know in Massachusetts — who sees herself as a professional, with a clear methodology to cleaning a home, a certificate in green cleaning and 28 years of experience — takes pride in the work she does but barely takes home enough to provide for herself and her son. Culturally, we value work that happens in the home less, and politically, we have excluded this workforce from equal protection in our labor laws for generations.

Fortunately, the growing social movement of low-wage workers, from domestic workers to restaurant workers, from fast food to retail, is organizing to change our culture and our laws, to disrupt these broader patterns of incquality. By supporting efforts to raise wages and improve the quality of low-wage jobs — beginning with the jobs historically associated with women and women of color — we can promote equity from the bottom up, ensuring that all working women are valued, and paid well enough to support their families.

How to Close a Gender Gap: Let Employees Control Their Schedules

BY CLAIRE CAIN MILLER | FEB. 7, 2017

THE MAIN REASON for the gender gaps at work — why women are paid less, why they're less likely to reach the top levels of companies, and why they're more likely to stop working after having children — is employers' expectation that people spend long hours at their desks, research has shown.

It's especially difficult for women because they have disproportionate responsibility for caregiving.

Flexibility regarding the time and place that work gets done would go a long way toward closing the gaps, economists say. Yet when people ask for it, especially parents, they can be penalized in pay and promotions. Social scientists call it the flexibility stigma, and it's the reason that even when companies offer such policies, they're not widely used.

A new job search company, Werk, is trying to address the problem by negotiating for flexibility with employers before posting jobs, so employees don't have to.

All the positions listed on the Werk site, including some from Facebook, Uber and Samsung, are highly skilled jobs that offer some sort of control over the time and place of work. People can apply to jobs that let them work away from the office all the time or some of the time, and at hours other than 9-to-5, part time or with minimal travel.

Another option gives workers the freedom to adjust their schedules, no questions asked, because of unpredictable obligations, like a sleepless night with a toddler or a trip to the emergency room with an older parent.

"Nobody wants to be the female in the department who says, 'My kid threw up on me this morning; I can't come in,'" said Annie Dean, who worked as a lawyer before starting Werk with Anna Auerbach, a former consultant. "Eighty percent of companies say they offer flexibility, but it's a black market topic. You raise it and you're not taken seriously."

Erin Fahs, 33, works from her home in Fort Myers, Fla., while her daughter Amelia, 2, plays. She found the job through Werk, a job site for skilled employees who want control over where and when they work.

For now, Werk is a limited experiment. Most of the employers are small companies, and it is aimed at an elite group of women — highly educated and on a leadership track. But it could provide lessons for how to improve work and make it more equal for a broader group.

Women who have less education or are paid hourly wages have significantly less flexibility than professional women to begin with. It makes working and caregiving that much harder.

Motherhood presents a different challenge for the elite women that Werk was made for. The careers that pay the most and require the most education, like business and law, also have the most gender inequality. Why? Economists have found it's a result of the long hours and limited flexibility. When educated mothers leave their jobs, it's often because they feel pushed out by inflexible employers, according to sociologists.

It's a big reason the top of corporate America is still so male; 4 percent of the chief executives of companies in the S.&P. 500 are women.

"They want top leadership roles," said Ms. Dean, who thought of the idea for Werk with Ms. Auerbach after they each had children. "The only reason they're not getting there is they're going through this phase in their life where working 16 hours at a single desk is incompatible with their life."

Seventy percent of working mothers say having a flexible work schedule is extremely important to them, according to a Pew survey. So do 48 percent of working fathers.

Workplace flexibility reduces turnover and work-family conflict, according to much of the research, including a study by 10 researchers from seven universities published in December. Yet when people get flexible work arrangements, they're generally isolated cases — for longtime employees whom companies trust and don't want to lose. The employers using Werk say they get access to highly skilled employees who might not otherwise apply.

Gerard Masci, founder and chief executive of Lowercase, a start-up eyeglass maker in Brooklyn, just hired a vice president for communications on Werk. She works part-time and remotely, except for monthly in-person meetings. "I don't care if this week you work less if in a month you work more, and whether they work in the space or not is irrelevant," Mr. Masci said. "All I care about is the productivity in the end."

"The happier she is in her flexibility," he said, "the more engaged she's going to be in her work."

Erin Fahs turned to Werk after her husband was transferred to Fort Myers, Fla., and she needed to find a new job. She wanted to work part time and from home because she was pregnant and the primary caregiver for their 2-year-old daughter. She found three jobs on Werk that would let her do that, and took one as the business manager for the Collective Good, which does consulting for nonprofits.

"Getting to have those direct conversations with the C.E.O. about what matters made it so much different from when I was applying for jobs earlier in my career," Ms. Fahs, 33, said.

She has a baby sitter 10 hours a week and works the other 10 hours when her daughter is sleeping. She has a few set meetings, which she attends via Google Hangouts — and gives her daughter an iPad for a diversion if there is a work emergency. She plans to expand to full-time work after maternity leave.

This type of flexibility, while valuable, would not magically solve workplace problems. For one, any solution would need to be for both women and men. Some jobs have to be done at a certain time and place, like teaching and food service. And even at companies where it's possible to let employees work at the time and place of their choosing, a different type of manager is required. Best Buy tried it for corporate employees, then revoked it.

"There are a vast number of jobs that could be handled in an own-your-schedule way, but it's just easier to measure performance by presence," said Anne-Marie Slaughter, the chief executive of the think tank New America, who has written about gender and work and advises Werk. "So it is a real adjustment for managers."

One Effort to Close the Gender Pay Gap Won't Get a Try Under Trump

BY CLAIRE CAIN MILLER | AUG. 31, 2017

THE OBAMA ADMINISTRATION had an idea it thought would help address the pay gap between white men and almost everyone else: requiring companies to report how much they paid people, along with their sex and race.

On Tuesday, that regulation became the latest of those reversed by the Trump administration, before the requirement was to go into effect next year.

Pay transparency, alone, would not have solved the pay gap problem. But without it, employees and regulators won't have evidence that a problem exists at any particular company — and employers will face less pressure to fix it.

There is little data on whether forcing companies to disclose pay makes it more equitable, mostly because the pay of individual workers or companies is generally kept secret. The Bureau of Labor Statistics surveys companies about compensation, but publishes only aggregate, anonymous data. Researchers who have studied the few instances in which companies have publicly disclosed individual salaries say it is not enough to close pay gaps, nor is it essential — some companies have closed them on their own, without publicly reporting pay information.

But most companies have no incentive to close pay gaps. The regulation provided that incentive — by pressuring them into it.

"Part of the motivation behind it would be to shame certain employers that found large gaps into doing something and taking proactive steps," said Jake Rosenfeld, a sociologist at Washington University in St. Louis who has studied the issue.

White women's median hourly earnings are 82 percent of those of white men, according to a Pew Research Center analysis of Bureau of Labor statistics data. Asian women earn 87 percent of what white men earn, while black women earn 65 percent and Hispanic women earn 58 percent. Black and Hispanic men also earn less than white men, while Asian men out-earn them.

The pay gap shrinks after controlling for factors like industry, education and hours worked, but a gap persists. Economists say the unexplained portion of the gap is probably because of discrimination.

The Obama regulation required that employers with at least 100 workers include aggregate, anonymous information about pay for categories of employees, on a form they already submit with information on sex, race and ethnicity. Similar policies are in effect in Europe, including a new law in Britain.

Proponents said the regulation would make it easier for employers to police themselves and harder for them to hide discrimination. It would also make it easier for the federal government to investigate them.

Business groups opposed the rule, saying it was a burden and wouldn't prove that any disparities were because of bias. The Trump administration agreed, and said it required too much paperwork.

While pay transparency doesn't prove discrimination, it's a starting point for employees and regulators to find out if there is any. Lilly Ledbetter, who inspired the Fair Pay Act of 2009, did not find out she was being paid less than men until she received an anonymous note 19 years after she started her job.

The little research that exists has shown that pay transparency leads to smaller pay gaps, sometimes just by making people aware there's an issue. Mr. Rosenfeld found in a study that it raised wages by helping workers negotiate. Many public-sector employers are required to publish pay, and pay gaps tend to be smaller.

Employers might not intentionally pay people differently, said Cynthia Estlund, a law professor at New York University who has written on the topic. But publishing the information highlights pay gaps that arise for other reasons, like the fact that women negotiate pay less often.

"These individual negotiation strategies with a lot of secrecy around salaries basically allow employers to keep salaries lower for some groups," she said.

Pay transparency can have unintended consequences. Though some research has found that it motivates people to work harder, other research has found that it lowers morale and motivates people to look for new jobs.

When California cities began publishing municipal salaries, one study found, it prompted pay cuts among men. The quit rate also increased by 75 percent.

A study by economists at Princeton and the University of California, Berkeley, found that people who were paid below the median reported lower job satisfaction and were more likely to look for new jobs, and that people who earned above the median reported no higher job satisfaction.

To get around the problem, some companies, like Salesforce, have done internal audits and given people raises to close the pay gap without publicizing pay. That might seem like the easiest solution — but companies are less likely to feel the need to do it without outside pressure.

How to Win the Battle of the Sexes Over Pay (Hint: It Isn't Simple.)

BY CLAUDIA GOLDIN | NOV. 10, 2017

WHEN BILLIE JEAN KING won the United States Open singles tennis title in 1972, her reward was a meager $10,000. Ilie Năstase, her male counterpart, won $25,000.

Ms. King fought hard for equal rights and, on the tennis court, she won. By 1973, men and women received the same prizes at the Open. That still can't be said of all tennis tournaments, but despite some ill-natured male grousing recently, equal pay is still the rule at the United States Open, at least.

That is not the reality in the overall labor market, however, where women still earn less than men and there is considerable confusion about the reasons for the gender earnings gap — and about what can be done to eliminate it.

Fighting to eradicate discriminatory employment practices is absolutely needed, of course. I've spent many years studying this subject, and my research shows that unequal treatment in hiring and in the work setting is real and may be reflected in unequal pay.

Yet it is also true that the time demands of many jobs can explain much of the pay difference, a finding that has sobering implications. Eliminating the gender earnings gap will require changes in millions of households and thousands of individual workplaces.

Even defining the gender earnings gap isn't simple: It cannot be reduced to a single number, though it often is expressed that way. According to a commonly used measure adopted by the United States Census Bureau, women in 2016 earned 81 cents for each dollar earned by men, both working full-time.

This definition focuses on the annual income of the individual at the median — or middle — of the income distribution for men and for women. Another valid option is to focus on mean, or average, earnings.

Measured that way, the earnings gap is even greater. And there are many other measures.

The gap is larger among more educated people, for example, and varies according to occupation, often in big ways. Among college graduates, it is far larger in business, finance and legal careers than in science and technology jobs. In health care, it is larger when self-employment is high (think dentists) and much lower when professionals are mainly employees (think pharmacists).

What's more, the gap is a statistic that changes during the life of a worker. Typically, it's small when formal education ends and employment begins, and it increases with age. More to the point, it increases when women marry and when they begin bearing children.

Using the data that shows women earn 81 cents for each dollar earned by men, when the careers of recent college graduates start, the gap is much smaller: 92 cents for each male dollar. By the time college-educated women are 40 years old, they earn 73 cents.

Similar patterns appear using data for women and men who have earned master's degrees in business administration. Immediately after graduation, women earn 92 cents for each male dollar. A decade later they earn only 57 cents.

Correcting for time off and hours of work reduces the difference in the earnings between men and women but doesn't eliminate it.

On the face of it, that looks like proof of disparate treatment. It may seem understandable that when a man works more hours than a woman, he earns more. But why should his compensation per hour be greater, given the same qualifications? But once again, the problem isn't simple.

The data shows that women disproportionately seek jobs — including full-time jobs — that are more likely to mesh with family responsibilities, which, for the most part, are still greater for women than for men. So, the research shows, women tend to prefer jobs that offer flexibility: the ability to shift hours of work and rearrange shifts to accommodate emergencies at home.

Such jobs tend to be more predictable, with fewer on-call hours and less exposure to weekend and evening obligations. These advantages have a negative consequence: lower earnings per hour, even when the number of hours worked is the same.

Is that unfair? Maybe. But it isn't always an open-and-shut case. Companies point out that flexibility is often expensive — more so in some jobs than others.

Certain job characteristics have a big impact on the gender earnings gap. I have looked closely at these issues, including the extent to which workers are:

• Subject to strict deadlines and time pressure

• Expected to be in direct contact with other workers or clients

• Instructed to develop cooperative working relationships

• Assigned to work on highly specific projects

• Unable to independently determine their tasks and goals

Occupations with a lower level of these characteristics (like jobs in science and technology) show smaller gaps, corrected for hours of work. Occupations with a higher level (like those in finance and law) have greater gaps. Men's earnings tend to surge when there are fewer substitutes for a given worker, when the job must be done in teams and when clients demand specific lawyers, accountants, consultants and financial advisers. Such differences can account for about half the gender earnings gap.

These findings provide more nuance in explaining why the gap widens with age and why it is greater for women with children. Whatever changes have already taken place in American society, the duty of caring for children — and for other family members — still weighs more heavily on women. And if you thought that moving to a more family-friendly nation would eliminate the gap, think again. In several nations, including Sweden and Denmark, a "motherhood penalty" in earnings exists, even though these nations have generous family policies, including paid family leave and subsidized child care.

Such considerations bring us to a very sensitive area: domestic arrangements at home, especially among couples with children. These are personal questions. In theory, gender earnings equality is possible when both parents take off the same amount of time and enjoy the same flexibility at work.

Yet this isn't easy to accomplish in the world, as it exists now: Individual families that make such choices may incur high costs. From a classic economic standpoint, if one spouse or partner can earn more by working less flexible hours, as a family, the couple would earn more money by having that parent in that job, while the other partner accepts the more flexible one. A man can certainly be the more flexible member of this household — though he typically is not. Such decisions need to be made couple by couple.

Reorganizing the workplace — a complicated undertaking — would help diminish the gap. It would also be narrowed if the burdens of family life were shouldered more equitably. In sum, the gap is mainly the upshot of two separate but related forces: workplaces that pay more per hour to those who work longer and more uncertain hours, and households in which women have assumed disproportionately large responsibilities.

Equality on this court requires a level playing field at home and in the market. There are many battles ahead. Unfortunately, they need to be fought at several levels.

CLAUDIA GOLDIN is a professor of economics at Harvard University.

How Boston Is Trying to Close the Gender Pay Gap

BY ANNA LOUIE SUSSMAN | MAY 26, 2018

THROUGH PAY-NEGOTIATION workshops and partnerships with more than 100 companies, the city is trying to help female workers match the salaries of male counterparts.

On a cold, sunny morning in April, Boston's mayor, Martin J. Walsh, took the podium in front of an audience of 150 corporate executives who had gathered at a downtown hotel to learn how men can be better allies to women at work. He quickly launched into one of his favorite stories, about a woman who approached him in an elevator to thank him for her recent $20,000 pay raise.

The kicker: He's not her boss. Instead, the woman got her raise after taking one of the free salary negotiation workshops that Boston has provided for women since 2016.

What happens when an entire city tries to close the gender pay gap? In the last few years, Mr. Walsh has doubled down on a commitment made in 2013 by his predecessor, Thomas M. Menino, to bring pay equity to the city's workforce. The Boston Women's Workforce Council teams up with the area's companies and institutions, including major ones like Morgan Stanley, Zipcar and the Massachusetts Institute of Technology, to help them figure out ways to advance women, which they share with one another in quarterly best-practice meetings.

The city has also trained over 7,000 women in salary negotiation, with a goal of training an additional 78,000 by 2021. A more immediate deadline: The Massachusetts Equal Pay Act, passed by the legislature in 2016, goes into effect in July.

The law states that "no employer shall discriminate in any way on the basis of gender in the payment of wages, or pay any person in its employ a salary or wage rate less than the rates paid to its employees of a different gender for comparable work." In addition, it prohibits employers from disciplining workers for discussing their salaries with colleagues or asking job applicants for their salary history.

(Massachusetts is not the first state to pass a pay equity law. In recent years, many states have been working to pass or strengthen their laws, including North Dakota, Illinois and Oregon. But none of those states has gone quite as far as Massachusetts.)

With employers, workers and policy all working toward the same goal, Boston is trying to succeed in an arena where decades of advocacy, research and good intentions have failed.

"If we just had the legislation, and employers weren't acting and women weren't asking, then it's going to close the gap a little bit but not enough," said Megan Costello, executive director of the Mayor's Office of Women's Advancement. "It has to be all of these things together."

A report last year by the Boston Women's Workforce Council, a public-private partnership, examined data from 114 companies that have pledged to close any pay gaps in their firms, covering 16 percent of the workers in the city, or nearly 167,000. It showed that women earned an average of $73,327 to men's $97,062, or 76 cents to the male dollar, less than the national average of about 80 cents. (As with recently released pay data from Britain, the gap can be partly explained by the higher concentration of men in senior roles.)

If progress in closing the pay gap over the past five decades continues at the same rate, women in the United States will not reach pay parity until 2059, the Institute for Women's Policy Research has calculated.

But people in Boston say change in their city may come earlier. "Four years ago, we had 37 companies, and we were struggling to get to 60," Ms. Costello said, referring to workshop participants. "Now we're at 223."

"Now, instead of whispering about it, we're actually talking about it," said Ashley Paré, a career coach and negotiation expert who leads salary negotiation workshops in Boston on a volunteer basis.

Megan Costello is executive director of the Mayor's Office of Women's Advancement, which is working with Boston-area employers to try to reduce pay inequity between women and men.

'IT LOOKS LIKE YOU'RE NOT A TEAM PLAYER'

On a recent April night at a Back Bay co-working space, around the corner from the tony shops of Newbury Street, Ms. Paré and her co-facilitator, Danielle Lucido, walked a group of 16 women through the basics of negotiation. Ms. Paré, who volunteers as part of Work Smart, a nationwide program administered by the American Association of University Women, started by reminding them that companies had good business reasons to treat female employees fairly.

"Companies are aware, especially now with #MeToo, and all these movements for equality," she told the audience, whose members ranged in age from the early 20s to late 40s. "Companies have to do the right thing, because talent is not going to stay with them."

A 49-year-old woman who works at a national telecommunications company was there, she said, because she recently discovered that a new male employee who works under her and is 11 years her junior makes $6,000 a year more than she does. She added that she had attended, in part, to share her story with younger women.

"I'm a real world example," said the woman, who did not want to be identified because, she said, she feared retribution from her employer.

She told the group that she had raised the issue with a manager two months ago, but that it had not yet been resolved. Instead, the manager told her, "Don't lose hope," she recounted, to supportive laughs.

Other participants were preparing to switch jobs and would be negotiating offers soon. Several said they worked at nonprofit organizations, where tight budgets were always an excuse not to pay more.

Over the next two hours, they discussed the origins of the pay gap and learned how to identify a target salary through market research on sites like Salary.com. They also embarked on a group job application and negotiation on behalf of "Olivia Taylor," a fictitious budding public relations executive whose case study is featured in the 32-page Work Smart workbook that every participant received.

Ashley Paré, left, and Danielle Lucido lead salary negotiation workshops in Boston. "Companies have to do the right thing, because talent is not going to stay with them," Ms. Paré told a recent gathering of women who believed they were being underpaid compared with their male peers.

The night was peppered with the knowing nods, empathetic laughs and "mm-hmms" that often characterize all-female gatherings, as women shared personal stories and insights.

Ms. Paré wanted to know: What are the main challenges holding women back from asking? A lack of information, one participant offered. Worrying about how you sound, said another. "But why," Ms. Paré asked, "would asking for more money damage a relationship with a boss?"

"It looks like you're not a team player," one woman in the back suggested.

"If you're a woman, yeah," another chimed in, to laughs from the room.

For the final exercise, a role-playing session, the women split into employer-employee pairs to practice the techniques they had learned.

"Employers" were given a maximum of $84,000 to offer in salary, while potential hires were told that their target was a minimum of $78,000. Most pairs made a deal, with salaries ranging from $80,000 to the maximum, with a signing bonus.

Caroline Roers, 23, works at a public relations agency, recently got a promotion with a pay raise but felt that she hadn't been able to negotiate successfully for specific benefits she wanted.

"It was interesting to hear the employer's perspective," Ms. Roers said. During negotiations, she said, "I'm so caught up in what I want and what my desires are that I don't think of 'Well, O.K., this is an employer and they have wants and desires.' "

With that in mind, she said, she was planning to look more closely at when her agency landed new accounts and clients, in order to determine when to make her next ask.

EXPANDING THE BASE

Boston was the first city to officially team up with the American Association of University Women, which now also offers Work Smart training in Tempe, Ariz.; Washington, D.C.; San Francisco; Long Beach, Calif.; and other locations in Massachusetts. The group says it plans to train 10 million women nationally in salary negotiation by 2022, with the addition of an online Work Smart course in English and Spanish, said Kimberly Churches, its chief executive officer, who noted that 39 states had equal pay legislation under consideration this year.

But she acknowledged that Boston's workshops had so far mostly reached salaried professionals with more education than the city's female work force as a whole.

"As successful as it was," Ms. Churches said, "we also needed to make sure we were emphasizing pockets of the city where there were increased numbers of women of color and of hourly wage earners, so we didn't just create even greater disparity in socioeconomic status."

For Hispanic women, the wage gap widens to 54 cents for every dollar earned by a white man, and for black women it's about 63 cents, based on median annual earnings, according to the Institute for Women's Policy Research.

A report on the first year's results recommended advertising in Spanish, Haitian Creole and other languages to reach minorities, and working through channels such as faith-based organizations or community health centers, to reach women outside industry groups.

Since January, the city has diversified both the participants and facilitators by increasing the number of workshops held outside downtown by 20 percent; holding them at 11 branches of the Boston Public Library, with more in the works; and working with organizations such as We, Ceremony, a visual storytelling platform for minority women, and the Latina Circle, a professional network.

Over half of the 166,705 employees whose employers submitted pay data to the Boston Women's Workforce Council are "professionals," compared with 32 percent in Greater Boston as a whole, according to the council's 2018 report. In part, that's because many of the companies that have signed on are in the financial, insurance, health care, pharmaceutical, engineering and nonprofit sectors. Companies that sign the pledge, known as the 100% Talent Compact, commit to submitting salary data every two years.

But some have joined the council precisely because they need more women. April's quarterly event on male allies featured two representatives from the construction industry, which is about 9 percent female, according to the National Association of Women in Construction. David Margolius, a project executive at Shawmut Design and Construction, and Robert Petrucelli, president and chief executive of Associated General Contractors of Massachusetts, spoke alongside Paul Francisco, chief diversity officer at State Street, a financial services firm.

Mr. Petrucelli said he that he had initially insisted to his group's communications director, Lisa Frisbie, that it didn't need a women's committee, especially since two women had chaired the organization's board in recent years and a number of women were active on and leading its other committees.

"I said: 'Why do you need a women's committee? Let the women join our committees, get integrated in,' " Mr. Petrucelli said. But, he added, Ms. Frisbie and Stacy Roman, another woman in the industry, who would eventually chair the women's committee, told them why they felt it was necessary.

"I heard from Lisa and Stacy Roman, 'No, you don't know how difficult it is, Bob, because you don't understand that we're operating in a vacuum, and we're all disconnected,' " he said.

The Building Women in Construction Committee is now the organization's fastest-growing committee.

"If it's one advice I can give my peers, it's listen," Mr. Petrucelli said. "Just listen, listen, listen, because the times they are a-changing."

Mr. Petrucelli said his eight-person organization had eliminated the distinction between "executive" staff, who were mostly men, and the mostly female "administrative" staff. He realized one female employee's responsibilities had outgrown her compensation, and gave her a 20 percent raise, bringing her in line with a similarly situated male employee.

Other employers that signed up reported making similar one-time pay increases, although few described them to employees as raises designed to correct historical gender or racial discrimination.

"We sort of expressed it more as a market adjustment," said Bob Rivers, chief executive of Eastern Bank, which has 1,900 employees, 68 percent of them women.

Eastern Bank now publishes salary ranges for different roles internally so employees can see where they stand. But Mr. Rivers said many of his peers were reluctant to submit their data to the city, and used that as a reason not to sign the pledge.

"You'll hear all myriad of excuses," he said. "One is around the data, the security of the data, the confidentiality of the data. Now, there are very large companies that have submitted, so that's a red herring."

CHAPTER 5

The Pay Gap Abroad

America is not the only country struggling to overcome the pay gap. In fact, gender-based pay inequality persists across most western nations. In 2017, this issue was crystallized when the BBC released the salary statistics of its top-paid employees. The data showed that only one-third of the top earners were women and just a handful were minorities. The outcry that followed resulted in a debate that reached across Europe. The articles in this section show how the pay gap is being confronted in Australia, Iceland, Scandinavia, Germany and Britain.

Wage Gaps for Women Frustrating Germany

BY SARAH PLASS | SEPT. 2, 2008

FRANKFURT — Maria Schaad, an ambitious 41-year-old businesswoman, considers herself lucky. After the birth of each of her sons, now 7 and 3, her employer, a major pharmaceutical company, allowed her to work flexible, reduced hours — a perk that is far from a given in Germany.

But her luck extended only so far: though Ms. Schaad had once set her sights on a position in management, her career stagnated after she started a family, she said, even though she had earned an M.B.A. after she became a mother.

"At some point, women have to make a decision," she said matter-of-factly. "Having children means you have to make compromises" at work.

Millions of working mothers — and sometimes fathers — have to make often difficult trade-offs when it comes to work and family, but labor experts say the calculus is especially harsh in Germany, a country that despite having a woman chancellor and sitting at the center of supposedly liberal Europe, has one of the widest gender wage gaps on the Continent.

It is just one of the disparities between working men and women, especially mothers, that government and union leaders say is creating a drag on female participation in the work force and, consequently, on economic growth, at a time when Germany may be teetering on the edge of recession. And they point to a range of societal and governmental barriers that are hindering change.

Ingrid Sehrbrock, deputy chairwoman of the German Federation of Trade Unions, calls German pay inequity a "scandal." Europe's commissioner for employment and social affairs, Vladimir Spidla, recently called on German employers "to really apply the principle of equal pay for equal work."

A clutch of new data suggests that Germany is going in the opposite direction. While the wage gap between women and men is narrowing across the European Union and in the United States, it is stagnant in Germany.

Since 2000, German working women on average have gone from earning 26 percent less than men to making 24 percent less than men in 2006, the last year for which statistics are available, according to data provided by the government statistics bureau, Destatis.

It is one of the largest gender gaps in the European Union. Only Cyprus, Estonia and Slovakia have equal or greater gaps, according to a study by the European statistics service, Eurostat.

Across the Continent, women on average made 15.9 percent less than men in 2007. That gap has narrowed each year since 2001, when women made 20.4 percent less than men, according to a report released last week by the European Union foundation that has studied the trend for years.

Comparing statistics with those of the United States can be difficult, since Europeans tend to count part-time and full-time workers, while the United States statistics most closely watched count only full-time workers. Women are more likely to work part time, which depresses their average wage and increases the gender gap when both full- and part-time workers are considered.

Still, the Census Bureau reported Tuesday that in 2007 American women working full time made 22 percent less than men working full time. It is the closest American women have ever come to income parity, a percentage point closer than in 2006. Since 2001, the number has bounced between 23 percent and 24.5 percent.

There are many reasons that Germany has continually been in the European cellar. Outright gender discrimination is one, researchers say. Maternity leave is another: men get promoted while their female colleagues take time off to have children.

"The dilemma is that while 50 percent of the junior employees are female, they pretty much disappear on their way to middle management," said Heiner Thorborg, a human resources consultant in Frankfurt and a vocal critic of gender inequality. The income gap is smaller for younger women who have not had children. It is greatest in western Germany, largely because the average hourly wage for men in this part of the country is almost 50 percent more than for men in the former East Germany.

Some human resources experts even point to less aggressive salary negotiations by women. (Coaching programs aimed at women have mushroomed over the last decade.)

But there are also societal and policy pressures. For example, mothers who work are sometimes derided as Rabenmutter, or "raven mothers." The phrase — based on the erroneous belief that ravens fly away, leaving their nests behind — refers to women who pursue careers instead of being homemakers. It is more common in the west than in the east of the country.

On the policy front, Germany has some of Europe's least generous supports for working parents. Just 9 percent of children age 3 or younger have access to day care, compared with an average of 23 percent in advanced countries. In northern European countries, the numbers are even higher: 40 to 60 percent.

East Germany still benefits from a wider network of child care operations — a legacy of the Communist era, when female participation in the work force was among the highest in the world and day care was vital.

The minister for family affairs, Ursula von der Leyen, recently introduced a plan to help finance private child care and increase the availability of kindergarten spots. The Parliament is expected to approve it by the end of the year.

Officials in Berlin have also tried to make having children more attractive. In 2007, the government introduced Elterngeld, or parents' money, a benefit intended to encourage fathers and mothers to take time off after the birth of a child. Almost 20 percent of new fathers have applied for the benefit so far this year.

Meanwhile, some 60 percent of married couples with children younger than 3 follow the same pattern: fathers keep working full time, while mothers stay at home.

The difficulty for many women in working and rearing children is partly responsible for Germany having one of Europe's lowest fertility rates: 1.37 children per woman, researchers say. It does not help that women in child-bearing years are still often asked in job interviews if they plan to have children — a question that is against the law.

Silke Strauss said she could not have attained her present position had she decided to have children. She was just named managing partner of a management consulting firm, and is the only female partner among eight men. "It would simply not work with children, not with the amount of flexibility that is expected," said Ms. Strauss, 42.

For some women, time spent abroad makes a critical difference, showing them that life can be different.

Jutta Allmendinger, the first female president of the Social Science Research Center in Berlin and the mother of a 14-year-old son, earned a Ph.D. at Harvard. While there, Ms. Allmendinger said, she saw the "idols of her youth" — female colleagues who taught while being pregnant and went back to work soon after giving birth, while still nursing their children.

Back in Germany in 1993, she became pregnant while teaching sociology in Munich. Some of her colleagues, unable to imagine she would consider having a baby, thought she had just overeaten during the summer. "It was impossible for some people that women in certain positions would actually have children," said Ms. Allmendinger, 51, laughing.

Those lucky enough to find a kindergarten or nursery school face yet another obstacle: many end the day at 3 p.m. or 4 p.m. — not very convenient for working mothers. That is one reason every third woman in Germany with a job works part time, the ultimate career killer, in the view of many human resources experts. Among Europeans, only women in the Netherlands have a higher share of part-time work.

About 61.4 percent of American working women worked full time and year-round in 2007, a record high — up from 60.6 percent in 2006, according to the census.

In a just-completed study, Ms. Allmendinger found that young women — and their male peers — want both a career and children.

Ms. Schaad, the pharmaceutical company employee, said those young women had better hurry. In business, she said, "Realistically, a woman who has not made it by 40 has no chance to make it at all."

Equal Pay for Men and Women? Iceland Wants Employers to Prove It

BY LIZ ALDERMAN | MARCH 28, 2017

REYKJAVIK, ICELAND — On a chilly afternoon in October, Frida Ros Valdi-marsdottir, a former home-care worker turned women's rights advo-cate, left her office at exactly 2:38 p.m. and headed to Reykjavik's main square, where throngs of women were forming a boisterous crowd. It was the time — roughly two and a half hours before the end of the workday — that many protesters reckoned they stopped being paid for equal work.

The rally was part of a groundswell for income equality that galva-nized tens of thousands of women across this tiny island nation, where protests often produce change.

"For decades, we've said we're going to fix this," said Ms. Valdi-marsdottir, the chairwoman of the Icelandic Women's Rights Asso-ciation and an organizer of the demonstration. "But women are still getting lower pay, and that's insane."

The government wants to change that dynamic. Iceland on Tuesday became the first country to introduce legislation requiring employers to prove they are paying men and women equally.

Iceland has had equal pay laws for half a century, pushing com-panies and the government to gradually reduce the pay gap. But the thinking behind the new legislation is that unless the laws are applied more forcefully, the imbalance may never really close.

"We want to break down the last of the gender barriers in the workplace," said Thorsteinn Viglundsson, Iceland's social affairs and equality minister. "History has shown that if you want progress, you need to enforce it."

Iceland, with a population of 330,000, is a forerunner in promoting gender equality. Nordic countries lead most other nations in equality policies that include gender quotas on boards and generous parental

Anna Kristin Kristjansdottir is an owner of the White House ad agency, where she is aiming to achieve gender parity in upper management.

leave, and Iceland consistently appears at or near the top of international rankings for fairness.

Yet equality in pay and inclusion in the upper ranks of the workplace have lagged. Women in Iceland still earn 14 percent to 20 percent less than men, according to the government.

Iceland wants to bridge the gap within five years, a move the government argues may speed progress in other areas. The global gender pay gap will not close for 70 years unless such efforts accelerate, according to the International Labor Organization.

The proposed legislation follows an equal pay pilot program in which government bodies and companies identified chronic hurdles that block women from higher-paying jobs: Women occupy different professions from men and fewer high-level positions, contributing to lower pay. Some employers in the program are now seeking to hire more women for jobs traditionally held by men.

Ms. Valdimarsdottir, the women's rights advocate, quit her home-care job for the municipality of Reykjavik.

She had discovered that an accountant for the municipality was paid four times as much as Ms. Valdimarsdottir was for her management role overseeing a 10-person team providing home care services, comprising mostly women. Later, the city adjusted the salary for her former position to be nearly equal with the accountant's, and raised salaries for the other workers.

Many Icelandic companies already embrace a voluntary equal pay standard forged by business organizations and labor unions. But business groups say it should not be imposed, particularly given the administrative burden of compliance, especially for small firms.

"Companies should do this for their own benefit and the benefit of their employees," said Halldor Thorbergsson, the director general for the Confederation of Icelandic Employers. "But it should not be legalized."

Businesses in other countries are also wary of government intervention, including in Britain, which recently required companies with 250 employees or more to publicly report their gender pay differences. Austria and Belgium have similar rules. In the United States and Switzerland, federal contractors must report wage information by gender to the government.

Icelandic women have long argued that equality needs a national push.

In 1974, 90 percent of women walked off jobs and out of their homes to show how society would be affected if they did not work. That watershed moment soon led to the world's first democratically elected female president, Vigdis Finnbogadottir, in 1980.

Today, about half of Iceland's Parliament members are women. Nearly 80 percent of women work and, with a gender quota in place, almost half of company board members are women.

Yet many women still have less economic power than men. Top level and intermediate managers are mostly men, and the pay gap is especially persistent for working mothers and women in female-dominated fields.

The new rules would require the biggest companies and government agencies to undergo audits, starting in 2018, and to obtain a certification of compliance with equal pay rules. Businesses with over 25 employees must comply by 2022.

Employers must assess every job, from cleaner to senior executive, to identify and fix wage gaps of more than 5 percent.

Although the process requires time and money, Arni Kristinsson, the managing director of BSI Iceland, a standards auditor that performs some of the fair pay reviews, said those costs were not insurmountable.

"The question is, are companies committed?" he said. "At firms that are, we are already seeing the pay gap narrow" to as little as 3 percent.

The audits revealed other workplace inequalities linked to pay. At the Icelandic Customs agency, which participated in the pilot program,

BARA KRISTINSDOTTIR FOR THE NEW YORK TIMES

In the tax department of the Icelandic Customs agency, most jobs are held by women and only a few by men.

officials found that salaries were lower when women were employed as a large group.

About 80 percent of Iceland's uniformed customs agents are men, a group paid 30 percent more than customs tax collectors, who are mostly women. The agents work longer hours and face challenges like inspecting cargo for drugs, so the review found the pay system was justified, said Snorri Olsen, Iceland's Customs director. But the review also spurred a reassessment of the gender balance in each group.

The agency is now trying to recruit more men for office work and more women into the higher-paid agent jobs, partly by shortening shifts to accommodate women who have child care demands, Mr. Olsen said.

"There's a tendency to look at work usually done by men as more valuable," he said. "This is technically a discussion of equal pay, but it's really a question about equality in our society."

The audits help promote self-reflection, even among female managers, about the potential for unconscious bias anywhere.

At a Reykjavik-based ad agency called the White House, Anna Kristin Kristjansdottir, a board member and owner, said the equal pay audit revealed leanings in the 45-person work force, including the proportion of higher-level jobs held by men. Like the Customs agency, she is seeking to even the percentages, especially in upper management, where she aims to achieve gender parity.

Whether such adjustments work are debatable. Some studies show pay gaps between men and women reside largely within occupations, not between them.

Equally disturbing to Ms. Kristjansdottir was that women negotiated lower salaries than men. Generally, men are four times as likely to ask for a raise, and when women ask, they seek 30 percent less on average.

"You'd be sitting there doing the interview, and they'd ask for less," Ms. Kristjansdottir said. "The audit showed this was a flaw in our recruitment, that we were allowing this to happen and didn't quite realize it."

For Mr. Viglundsson, the government official, the fact that larger equality issues surface in the debate over equal pay is justification enough for the legislative proposal.

"When it comes to the workplace, men have enjoyed a certain level of privilege for a long time," he said. "But if you look at the vested interests for society of eliminating discrimination against women, that far outweighs any regulatory burden."

Australian TV Host's Departure Raises Questions on Gender Pay Gap

BY JACQUELINE WILLIAMS | OCT. 17, 2017

SYDNEY, AUSTRALIA — For decades she has blazed a trail in the Australian media, bringing the news to homes around the country. But on Monday, Lisa Wilkinson herself became the subject of the day's breaking news, her resignation reigniting a fierce debate about a gender pay gap, an issue that has increasingly roiled the media industry. "I'm sad to say that today was my last day on 'The Today Show,' " Ms. Wilkinson wrote on Twitter late Monday, referring to Nine Network's flagship breakfast program, which she had co-hosted for a decade.

Her post contained a statement from the network confirming the split, which came after months of contract negotiations. "We have been unable to meet the expectations of Lisa Wilkinson and her manager on a contract renewal for a further period," the network statement said, adding that it was "disappointed we find ourselves in this position."

News of her abrupt departure set off speculation that Ms. Wilkinson, 57, had quit over an equal pay dispute. She had for 10 years been a co-host alongside Karl Stefanovic and at times had fended off questions about a pay gap between the two.

Australian news outlets have reported that Mr. Stefanovic was paid nearly twice as much as Ms. Wilkinson. Ms. Wilkinson, who is also the editor at large for HuffPost's Australian arm, has not responded to requests for comment.

Within an hour of announcing her split from Nine Network, Ms. Wilkinson revealed that she had been snapped up by the rival Network Ten, which is being purchased by the CBS Corporation, the American broadcaster.

She will join "The Project," Network Ten's top news and current affairs program, starting next year, Ten said. The deal could make her the highest-paid female host on Australian television, local news reports said.

Her departure comes as other news outlets have been facing questions about gender pay disparities. In July, the BBC released pay data showing that women represented only one-third of the on-air talent who were paid at least 150,000 pounds, or about $200,000, by the broadcaster in the past year.

Ms. Wilkinson's move drew praise from leading women across the media industry.

"What a woman. Lisa Wilkinson taking a stand for women everywhere by asking for equal pay with her co-host and walking when Channel Nine refused," wrote Mia Freedman, co-founder of the women's media company Mamamia. "Now she has a better deal at Channel 10."

Her departure from Nine Network also drew the attention of prominent politicians.

"If the reason is about equal pay, I say good on her," said Gladys Berejiklian, the premier of New South Wales. "I think she's sending a very strong message to the community."

Nine Network acknowledged Ms. Wilkinson's contribution to "The Today Show," saying that her partnership with Mr. Stefanovic had "taken the show to the success it is today."

The pair embodied the easygoing Australian character with lighthearted banter and moments of mutual appreciation, with Ms. Wilkinson playing the calm, composed foil to Mr. Stefanovic's regular tomfoolery.

Before hiring Ms. Wilkinson in 2007, Nine Network cycled through various co-hosts for Mr. Stefanovic to chip away at the popularity of "Sunrise," the long-dominant breakfast show on Seven Network.

After Ms. Wilkinson joined "The Today Show," its audience gradually increased, although not enough to overtake "Sunrise."

"It was a stunning turnaround for a program many had written off a decade earlier," wrote Michael Lallo, an entertainment reporter for Fairfax Media. "This should have been sufficient proof of Wilkinson's value."

Mr. Stefanovic opened the show Tuesday morning by acknowledging his shock at the departure of Ms. Wilkinson and thanking her for her support, citing "the laughs, sage advice, the calmness."

"For 10 years Lisa has dragged herself out of bed at 3:30 in the morning, fed the dogs and cats, put a load of washing on, and come into work and sat on my left to inform you at home about what's happening in the world," Mr. Stefanovic said.

Nine Network said it would be "going in another direction" and considering its options over "the coming weeks and months."

On Monday, Ms. Wilkinson was described by a fellow anchor, Leigh Sales of the Australian Broadcasting Corporation, as a "steady, consistent, highly competent, warm and delightful presence" on "The Today Show."

ADAM BAIDAWI contributed reporting from Melbourne, Australia.

Children Hurt Women's Earnings, but Not Men's (Even in Scandinavia)

BY CLAIRE CAIN MILLER | FEB. 5, 2018

Motherhood is the biggest cause of the gender pay gap. It might take fathers to change that.

SCANDINAVIA IS SUPPOSED to be a family-friendly paradise. We imagine fathers and mothers spending their children's early months together at home. Then they enroll them in high-quality, government-subsidized child care, from which they pick them up at the end of the world's shortest workdays.

But it is not as egalitarian as the fantasy suggests. Despite generous social policies, women who work full-time there are still paid 15 percent to 20 percent less than men, new research shows — a gender pay gap similar to that in the United States.

The main reason for this pay gap seems to be the same in both places: Children hurt mothers' careers. This is, in large part, because women spend more time on child rearing than men do, whether by choice or not.

A series of recent studies shows that in both the United States and Europe, the gender pay gap is much smaller until the first child arrives. Then women's earnings plummet and their career trajectories slow. Women who do not have children, by and large, continue to grow their earnings at a similar rate to men. There are still differences because of discrimination and other factors, but researchers say that motherhood explains a large amount of the gap.

It's another sign that in modern economies, with their two-income families and with a priority on long hours spent in the office, even countries with the most family-friendly policies haven't made things equal.

Policies like paid leave, subsidized child care and part-time work options are helpful to mothers. Scandinavia has one of the highest rates of women's labor force participation in the world, and the share of women working in the United States has fallen behind the share in Europe, which has much more generous policies.

But policy alone would not be enough to overcome gender inequality. It would require changes in behavior — including by men. There is evidence that the gap would shrink if fathers acted more the way mothers do after having children, by spending more time on parenting and the related responsibilities.

"At the very least, men have to take a larger role," said Francine Blau, an economist at Cornell who has studied the gender pay gap and family-friendly policies in the United States and Europe. "It does become a distinction in the eyes of employers between potential male and female workers, and it may reinforce traditional gender roles."

One new study, which used a data set including everyone in Denmark from 1980 to 2013, along with details about their jobs and families, found that while there was a pay gap before people had children, it was relatively small and earnings were increasing at similar rates. But after the first child, women's gross earnings quickly dropped 30 percent, and never fully recovered. In the long term, mothers earned 20 percent less. Women who did not have children continued to increase their earnings at a rate similar to men.

Most studies of the pay gap analyze equal pay for equal work. But in this paper, researchers examined how women changed their work in response to having children, and how that affected their lifelong pay. Mothers were paid less partly because they worked fewer hours, took longer breaks from employment and were more likely to move into lower-paying, family-friendly jobs, the paper found. Their probability of becoming a manager also declined.

"Equal work is in practice not an option for most women, because they have to take care of the children and therefore have different kinds of jobs and different kinds of hours," said Henrik Kleven, an economist at Princeton, who wrote the paper with Jakob Egholt Sogaard, an economist at the University of Copenhagen, and Camille Landais, an economist at the London School of Economics.

As in the United States, the pay gap in Denmark has shrunk over time as women have become better educated than men and more likely to be professionals or managers. Children, which accounted for 40 percent of the pay gap in 1980, now account for 80 percent of it. Discrimination and other factors play a role in the remaining gap, researchers say.

The same pattern is true elsewhere. In the United States, a study by Census Bureau researchers found that between two years before the birth of a couple's first child and a year after, the earnings gap between opposite-sex spouses doubles. The gap continues to grow for the next five years.

Two studies of college-educated women in the United States found that they made almost as much as men until ages 26 to 33, when many women have children. By age 45, they made 55 percent as much as men.

In Sweden, a recent study found, female executives are half as likely as men to be chief executives, and one-third less likely to be high earners — even when they were more qualified for these jobs than men. Most of the difference was explained by women who were working shorter hours and taking time off work in the five years after their first child was born.

As any parent knows, children come with a host of time-consuming responsibilities. Someone has to do the work. In most opposite-sex couples, that someone is the mother.

There are different explanations for this, researchers say. Women may have intrinsic preferences to do more of this work, or couples could decide it's most efficient to divide the labor this way. It could also be that social norms about traditional gender roles influence men and women to behave this way.

In surveys of Americans and Europeans, people tend to say that women should work part-time or not at all when they have children at home, and that men should earn money to support their families. The Denmark study found evidence that women took on the roles they saw their mothers take — those whose mothers worked more had smaller pay gaps themselves.

Policies have different effects on how people approach work and home responsibilities, researchers say. Very long paid maternity leave, which is common in Europe, increases the chances that women return to the labor force but decreases their pay and promotions, because they take such long breaks.

Subsidized child care helps shrink the pay gap by enabling women to spend more time working. There is also evidence that mothers whose employers let them work flexibly or telecommute are less likely to reduce their work hours.

But as long as mothers, and not fathers, are the ones using policies like paid leave and taking on the additional work at home after having children, the lifetime pay inequity seems certain to remain.

Research has shown that when men take care of their babies in the early weeks, they are more involved in child care years later. But while Denmark gives new parents a year off, and mothers and fathers can share most of it, men on average take only two weeks, Mr. Kleven said. Countries like Sweden have been able to increase the amount of paternity leave that fathers take with a policy incentive: Families in which each parent takes a certain amount of time off receive additional time off to add to their combined allowance.

"If you know that both men and women will go off and take care of children, not just women, what that does is remove the motherhood penalty," said Heejung Chung, a sociologist at the University of Kent.

British Companies Must Reveal How They Pay Women vs. Men

BY AMIE TSANG | APRIL 6, 2017

AT THE CURRENT RATE of progress, it could take nearly a century before the gender pay gap is closed in Britain. So the government is trying to speed up the process.

Putting pressure on employers to tackle the nation's gender pay gap, new rules taking effect on Thursday will require large companies to publish the average salaries of the men and the women they employ.

The regulation affects companies with 250 or more employees. The figures must reveal information like salary differences between men and women, differences in average bonuses and the proportion of men and women who received those bonuses.

The rules give the companies until April 2018 to report the information to the government and publish it on their websites and on a government website.

"Helping women to reach their full potential isn't only the right thing to do, it makes good economic sense and is good for British business," Justine Greening, the minister for women and equalities, said in a statement.

Under British law, men and women should receive equal pay for the same job, but there is still a gap between average wages when it comes to gender.

The gender pay gap in Britain was 18.1 percent in 2016, dropping from 27.5 percent in 1997, according to the Office for National Statistics.

The gap exists in large part because there are fewer women in senior roles and the women often do the jobs where pay is lower, said Jon Terry, a partner at the accounting firm PwC who advises financial clients on hiring and pay.

According to research by PwC, it would take 95 years to close the gender pay gap in countries in the Organization for Economic Cooperation and Development, of which Britain is a member.

Women's pay has become a more prominent topic in countries like Iceland and France, where women have walked out of their jobs at the hour they generally stopped being paid equally for their work.

In the United States, decades after President John F. Kennedy signed the Equal Pay Act, women earned 79 cents for every dollar men earned in 2014, according to the Census Bureau.

Social scientists say one way to effect change is to publish everyone's pay. Jake Rosenfeld, a sociologist at Washington University, found that salary transparency raised wages, in part because "even being cognizant of gender pay disparity" can change norms.

In New York, the City Council tackled the issue on Wednesday by voting to prohibit employers from asking job seekers about previous salaries to help "break the cycle of gender pay inequity by reducing the likelihood that a person will be prejudiced by prior salary levels."

In Britain, many hope the regulations will prompt companies to examine why the gender pay gap exists.

"It puts such a spotlight on the issue," Mr. Terry said. "It's easier to see whether an organization is taking this seriously."

Sam Smethers, the chief executive of the Fawcett Society, which campaigns for women's rights and equality, said the new regulation, passed by the British government in February, was the most significant legal change since the Equal Pay Act of 1970.

"It's the first time we require employers to look at their pay and report on that, so that is significant change," Ms. Smethers said.

There are doubts about how effective the regulation will be.

"There is no penalty for noncompliance," Ms. Smethers noted. "Not requiring an action is a real weakness. It's not just about the numbers; it's about engaging with the problem you've got."

Some companies say the numbers do not matter in the big scheme of things. Over a quarter of senior personnel interviewed for a survey in March by the consulting firm NGA Human Resources said the gender gap was not an issue for businesses.

And about 10 percent of the people interviewed said a plan was not necessary to address gender pay gap challenges in their organizations.

Even if these companies do not have a gender pay gap, it was surprising that they did not have a plan in place, said Geoff Pearce, a managing consultant at NGA.

"Businesses need to look at what the implications are," he said. "If it creates an issue, that can affect their ability to recruit and retain talent, and studies have shown that the more diverse a work force is, the more productive it is."

Still, the British regulation was likely to speed up change, Mr. Terry of PwC said; companies that do not grasp the value of reporting the salary information may be persuaded to take it seriously if their reputations are at stake and they are named and shamed.

"The gender pay reporting really smacks them in the face," he said. "If they have a pay gap of 18 percent, they will get a lot of negative press."

BBC Publishes Pay of Top Stars, Revealing Gender Gap

BY SEWELL CHAN | JULY 19, 2017

LONDON — Only one-third of the BBC's top-paid stars are women, and only a tiny number are black, Asian or members of another minority group, according to pay data that the publicly funded broadcaster published for the first time on Wednesday.

Like the National Health Service, the BBC is seen in Britain as a central institution of public life, but it is competing in a rapidly changing environment and faces growing demands for transparency and accountability.

The broadcaster is largely financed through an annual license fee of 147 pounds, or about $191, paid by nearly every British household, but it also receives commercial and other income, most of it generated from abroad.

Since 2009 the BBC had released the salaries of senior managers making at least £150,000, but last year the Conservative government demanded, as part of the renewal of the broadcaster's governing charter, that the BBC also disclose the pay above that level from license fee revenue to its on-air stars. (The prime minister, Theresa May, is paid just over £150,000 a year.)

The data began to dribble out Wednesday morning after the television personality Piers Morgan posted some of the figures on Twitter, in apparent violation of a journalistic embargo.

Although direct comparisons were difficult, because many of those named handle more than one assignment, the publication of the data, an annex to the organization's annual report, immediately prompted discussion about pay disparities. (The figures were released as pay bands, rather than as precise numbers.)

Tony Hall, the BBC's director general, said less than 0.25 percent of the broadcaster's 43,000 talent contracts last year involved annual pay of more than £150,000.

"On gender and diversity, the BBC is more diverse than the broadcasting industry and the Civil Service," Mr. Hall said, though he added that the disclosures highlighted "the need to go further and faster."

By 2020, the BBC intends for all "all our lead and presenting roles to be equally divided by men and women," he said. Of the top talent hired or promoted in the past three years, he said, more than 60 percent were women.

Mr. Hall said the BBC had set a "rough target" that called for 15 percent of its highest paid stars to be of minority backgrounds by 2020; of those hired or promoted in the last few years, nearly 20 percent belong to minorities.

Critics were not satisfied. Harriet Harman, a Labour Party member of Parliament, said the "lid has been lifted" on pay discrimination, citing an "old boys' network where they are feathering their own nests and each other's, and there is discrimination and unfairness against women."

The BBC has long faced criticism from commercial rivals who regard its prominent position as a bar to their ambitions.

Mr. Hall said the BBC was now competing for talent not only with broadcasters like ITV and Sky, but also with online media giants like Netflix, Amazon and Apple.

He cited research showing that BBC users overwhelmingly agreed that the organization should employ top actors and journalists "even if it means paying the market rate."

Gerry Morrissey, the leader of the labor union Bectu, which represents thousands of engineers, technical workers and other production staff who make a small fraction of what the on-air stars take home, called for a yearly minimum salary of £20,000.

The list revealed that Chris Evans, who hosts BBC Radio 2's breakfast show, was the highest-paid male celebrity, with a salary of at least £2 million. Claudia Winkleman, who hosts "Strictly Come Dancing," the British equivalent of "Dancing with the Stars," and BBC Radio 2's arts program, is the corporation's highest-paid female celebrity, earning between £450,000 and £499,999 (which also happens to be the pay range for Mr. Hall, the BBC chief).

Social media sites lit up with comments on what appeared to be pay disparities. For example, Laura Kuenssberg, the political editor of BBC News, makes £200,000 to £249,999, less than Nick Robinson, a BBC Radio 4 anchor and her predecessor in the role, who makes £250,000 to £299,999.

Gary Lineker, a former soccer star who now hosts the highly watched "Match of the Day" highlights program, earned £1.75 million to just under £1.8 million.

In contrast, the BBC's highest-paid female sports figure, Sue Barker, a former tennis champion who plays a lead role in the broadcaster's Wimbledon coverage, earned £300,000 to £349,999.

(Clare Balding, who also hosts Wimbledon coverage but who plays a more prominent role in BBC sports coverage throughout the year, took home £150,000 to £199,999 — putting her in the same pay band as John McEnroe, the American former tennis star, who provides occasional commentary on matches.)

Huw Edwards, one of the main anchors of the BBC's flagship "News at Ten," earned £550,000 to £599,999; Fiona Bruce, another main anchor, made about £200,000 less.

Some of the personalities came forward to defend their pay. Andrew Marr, an author and news broadcaster known for his hard-hitting political interviews, said in a statement that he was paid £400,475 a year — for "the weekly Sunday morning show, my radio work, documentary commissions, television obituaries, and work on big news events." Mr. Marr said his annual salary was £139,000 less than it had been two years ago.

Several stars of the long-running soap opera "EastEnders" were on the list. And the actor Peter Capaldi, who is in his final season as the star of the sci-fi series "Doctor Who," was paid more than £200,000 a year.

"The right has for a long time targeted the BBC as wasteful and inefficient, as part of its free-market agenda," said Tom Mills, a sociologist at Aston University in Birmingham, England, and the author of "The BBC: Myth of a Public Service." Top salaries at the broadcaster increased in the 1990s, he said, partly in response to pressure to make the BBC more commercial.

He said the BBC should consider a ceiling on salaries, perhaps based on a multiple of the salary of its lowest-paid workers. The high salaries, he said, contribute to a growing public feeling that the broadcaster is elitist.

Reporting was contributed by **STEPHEN FARRELL**, **PETER ROBINS**, **DES SHOE**, **AMIE TSANG** and **MICHAEL WOLGELENTER**.

BBC News Editor Quits Her Post to Protest Gender Pay Gap

BY MATTHEW HAAG | JAN. 7, 2018

A SENIOR EDITOR for BBC News accused the network in an open letter on Sunday of operating a "secretive and illegal" salary system that pays men more than women in similar positions.

The editor, Carrie Gracie, who joined the network 30 years ago, said she quit her position as China editor last week to protest pay inequality within the company. In the letter posted on her website, she said that she and other women had long suspected that their male counterparts drew larger salaries and that BBC management had refused to acknowledge the problem.

She said she decided to make her story public, risking discipline or dismissal, because she wanted viewers to know the BBC had been "resisting pressure for a fair and transparent pay structure."

"I simply want the BBC to abide by the law and value men and women equally," Ms. Gracie wrote, citing the Equality Act 2010, which states that men and women doing equal work must receive equal pay. "On pay, the BBC is not living up to its stated values of trust, honesty and accountability."

Her letter comes at a moment of reckoning for news media organizations in the United States and elsewhere, ushered in by the #MeToo movement that has revealed discrimination and sexual misconduct in an industry long dominated by men.

Her letter also magnified the pressure the BBC has recently faced internally and externally to fix a significant pay gap between men and women throughout its ranks, even among its top television and radio stars.

Ms. Gracie's letter was met with statements of support from several high-profile figures at the BBC, and she expressed her gratitude on Monday while hosting the flagship news program "Today" on BBC Radio 4.

The BBC did not respond to a request for comment on Sunday night but in a statement to BBC News, a spokeswoman, citing a salary audit, said there was "no systemic discrimination against women" and that "a significant number of organizations have now published their gender pay figures showing that we are performing considerably better."

Last year, the publicly funded network published the salary ranges of employees who earned more than £150,000, or about $204,000, annually — a list that was two-thirds men and included no women among its seven highest earners. Ms. Gracie did not make the list. On average, men made about 10 percent more than women, the report found.

Ms. Gracie said she learned in that report just how severely she had been underpaid despite her high-ranking position in its news division. While she did not reveal her salary, she said that of the four international news editors, the two men earned 50 percent more than the two women.

She wrote that she believed her promotion to China editor, which required her to move to Beijing and leave her children in the United Kingdom, meant she would be paid the same as her male colleagues.

"Like many other BBC women, I had long suspected that I was routinely paid less, and at this point in my career, I was determined not to let it happen again," she wrote about accepting the China editor position in 2014. "Believing that I had secured pay parity with men in equivalent roles, I set off for Beijing."

Ms. Gracie said that after the salaries were made public, she asked for pay matching her male counterparts'. BBC management offered her a "big pay rise which remained far short of equality," so she declined it, she wrote.

"Since turning down an unequal pay rise, I have been subjected to a dismayingly incompetent and undermining grievance process which still has no outcome," she added.

Ms. Gracie, who could not be reached on Sunday night, previously worked as a presenter on the BBC.

While she has quit her job in China, Ms. Gracie said she will return to a former position within the newsroom "where I expect to be paid equally," she wrote.

Britain Aims to Close Gender Pay Gap With Transparency and Shame

BY LIZ ALDERMAN | APRIL 4, 2018

THE GENDER PAY GAPS detailed by British companies in recent months surprised almost no one — men are paid more than women, often by a wide margin, at the vast majority of businesses.

But by making companies publicly air their salary information, Britain intends to force a reckoning. Officials in London hope the embarrassing revelations in the reports, which had to be submitted by Wednesday, will shame companies into doing more to close the divide.

The push is one of a growing number of efforts among countries to promote the principle of equal pay. Australia recently mandated gender pay gap reporting for most companies. In Germany, a new law will require businesses with more than 500 employees to reveal their pay gaps. Nordic countries like Iceland have been even more aggressive, by making companies prove they are paying male and female staff equally.

Proponents of the British effort argue that the increased transparency will lead to smaller gaps. Research by the accounting firm PwC predicts that if nothing is done, it could take nearly a century for the divide to close entirely across the Organization for Economic Cooperation and Development, a group of rich countries that includes Britain.

"This is a game-changer," said Andrew Bazeley, a policy manager at the Fawcett Society, a British organization that campaigns for women's rights and equality. "It will force businesses to think about the gender pay gap in ways they might not have before."

Under the new reporting requirements, companies with 250 or more employees must publish salary differences between men and women every year. They are also required to provide details on gaps in average bonuses paid, and the proportion of men and women who received those bonuses.

EasyJet headquarters at London Luton Airport. Men outearn women by around 52 percent at easyJet, which has pledged to hire more female pilots.

The submissions have made for uncomfortable reading for company executives. At Goldman Sachs's sprawling moneymaking machine in Britain, women are paid an average of 56 percent less than men. Men outearn women by around 52 percent at easyJet, the country's busiest discount airline. And at WPP, the British advertising giant, women take home, on average, around one-quarter less than their male counterparts.

Still, at least in some cases, the requirement to publish the data has made an impact as big companies have scrambled to counter the fallout from embarrassing reports. EasyJet has said its male chief executive would take a 4.6 percent pay cut to match the salary of his female predecessor, and pledged to more than triple the proportion of its female pilots.

In other cases, a change in the pay culture has been pushed from the outside. At Mills & Reeve, a British law firm whose audit determined it was paying women an average of 32 percent less than men, a major impetus has come from big clients that have started to request more female representation among the firm's attorneys.

"It's increasingly something we're asked for as part of tenders and pitches, to give details of our diversity," said Claire Clarke, a managing partner.

Some efforts predate the new rules, but have come into focus because of the requirements. The British bank Barclays, for example, has sought to hire, and retain, more senior female executives by offering a new 12-week "internship" targeted at experienced women who are coming off a career break and introducing greater flexibility in existing jobs.

Supporters of the British regulations acknowledge that transparency alone won't solve the problem. But without it, companies and regulators in countries seeking to enforce equal pay laws would have scant evidence that a gap existed — and face less pressure to address it. Jake Rosenfeld and Patrick Denice, sociologists at Washington University, found in a study that salary transparency raised wages, in part because "even being cognizant of gender pay disparity" helped change norms.

Such is the case in Iceland. The country has gone further than any other, becoming the first to require employers to submit to external audits to prove they are paying women on a par with men. The thinking was that unless equal pay laws were applied more forcefully, the imbalance might never close.

Iceland's government has vowed to completely close the nation's gender pay gap by 2022, after women walked out of their jobs en masse in protest on a chilly afternoon in October 2016.

The Icelandic initiative sought to address chronic hurdles that block women around the world from higher-paying positions. No matter the country, men often hold a disproportionately large number of high-level positions, while women — especially mothers — tend to populate lower-paying fields and jobs with more work-time flexibility to take care of families. After Iceland began enforcing pay audits, some employers sought to hire more women for jobs traditionally held by men.

The United States, by contrast, has taken a step backward on reporting. Last year, the Trump administration rolled back an Obama-era initiative that sought to create incentives to close pay gaps. The move would have required companies to report how much they paid workers based on gender and race, but the White House now says it would have posed a burden on employers.

Britain's rules, though tougher than efforts in the United States, fall short of the moves in Iceland.

They cover only about a third of all companies. Employers won't face penalties even if they report discrepancies year after year. And businesses are not required to address some of the biggest causes of the pay divide, including the lack of women in high-paid senior roles.

The gender pay gap in Britain is just over 18 percent, down from 27.5 percent in 1997, according to official data. But those figures are still likely to underestimate the real gap, critics say. An analysis of 1,000 British companies by DueDil, a company-information platform in London, showed that just 13 percent of women held top directorships, creating a "significant gender gap in senior leadership" and in average pay.

Still, even without stricter enforcement, the government is betting that the mere publication of pay data will shame companies into taking action, and provide employees with ammunition to press for greater pay equality.

To coincide with the deadline on Wednesday, British women started a #PayMeToo hashtag campaign on Twitter, encouraging employees to talk to one another about how much they are paid. The nascent effort, pushed by a group of female British lawmakers, seeks to encourage women to talk about their pay at work, and make clear what rights they have.

"If we are serious about tackling the gender pay gap, then we have to do more than publish data," Stella Creasy, a member of Parliament from the opposition Labour Party, said in an interview with The Guardian. "We have to show we're watching what happens next."

AMIE TSANG contributed reporting.

The Gender Pay Gap: Trying to Narrow It

BY AMIE TSANG AND LIZ ALDERMAN | MAY 13, 2018

LONDON — A law firm is giving female lawyers more flexible work schedules. A technology giant wants to increase the ranks of its female engineers. And a media company is recruiting greater numbers of women to mirror its client base more closely.

New rules in Britain requiring companies to publish the extent of their gender pay gap have spurred a far-reaching debate over inequality in the workplace. Businesses — the vast majority of which pay men more than women — are increasingly being shamed into action.

The hurdles are plentiful. Men hold most high-level roles. Women take more time out of work to look after children. Higher-paying sectors, like sales and those requiring technical skills, are dominated by men.

What, then, can be done?

MICHAEL HIRSHON

'ME AND 30 OTHER GUYS'

When Stella Worrall started working as a field technician last year at Virgin Media, she felt more than a little conspicuous.

More than 96 percent of the company's field technicians, who install the boxes and cables that deliver television and broadband services to people's homes, are men. Some of Virgin's technical sites did not even have women's bathrooms. And the environment could feel intimidating because there were simply no other women around.

"My training was me and 30 other guys," Ms. Worrall said. "It was quite daunting at first."

Virgin reported a median pay gap of 17.4 percent, meaning that women earned around 83 pounds for every 100 pounds earned by men (100 pounds is about $140). Women make up half the company's customers but only 29 percent of its staff, and female clients are increasingly requesting female field technicians to install Virgin's media services at home.

MICHAEL HIRSHON

When Stella Worrall was trained to be a field technician for Virgin Media, she was the only woman in a group of dozens.

To meet the demand, Virgin Media, a subsidiary of Liberty Global with about 13,000 employees, is widening its recruitment net. It has experimented with all-female sets of interns, and requirements to have one woman on every short list for a vacant job, said Catherine Lynch, Virgin Media's chief people officer.

The company has also sought to increase the proportion of senior women through mentoring and by encouraging women to apply for promotions. That has raised concerns that some women promoted were younger than usual or lacked experience in the departments they were moving into.

Ms. Lynch insists, however, that the moves will pay off.

At the moment, only a quarter of the highest-paid people in the company are women.

Ms. Worrall, who worked part time for several years, was promoted to technician after just eight weeks of training.

"We're trying to identify who might be the shining stars that we can fast-track a little bit with a bit more sponsorship," Ms. Lynch said.

"I don't think we'll always have to do that," she added. "There will come a tipping point where the momentum will have been created."

WORKING THE LAW

In 2015, Claire Clarke became the first female managing partner at Mills & Reeve, a British law firm. At the time, about 28 percent of the firm's partners were women.

In recent years, Mills & Reeve has tried to do a better job of recruiting and retaining women, in particular by promoting part-time work. The firm hoped that would help with the difficulty of juggling onerous working hours with motherhood.

It was an issue Ms. Clarke, the mother of four, had to deal with herself. "I have to go through the school calendars and schedule the parents' evenings, school concerts, sports days into my work calendar," she recounted.

Since Claire Clarke became her law firm's managing partner, changing the number of women at the top has been tough. Law firms must take "into account the needs of their clients," she said.

Despite the part-time push, Mills & Reeve has made little progress. Last year, in fact, the proportion of women who were partners at the firm was slightly lower than when Ms. Clarke started, creating a median gender pay gap of 34 percent.

It is a challenge mirrored in the industry. Women make up more than half of the solicitors at law firms in Britain, but only 28 percent of the partners, according to Britain's Law Society.

Several law firms offer part-time work. But the option is one used by about a third of the women at Mills & Reeve and 7 percent of the men.

Staff needs still have to be balanced with client demands.

For major law firms in Britain, clients often expect round-the-clock availability. Roles with more responsibility, and higher pay, often come with tough deadlines — whether for filing documents with a stock exchange or wrapping up the acquisition of a company.

Nearly half of all respondents to a survey for the Law Society said the profession required an unacceptable work-life balance to progress to senior ranks.

Working mothers, as a result, often default to one of three main options. They opt for more flexibility, which results in their working fewer hours than male counterparts; stick with areas of practice with fewer fast-moving transactions; or head for internal roles at corporations.

"Law firms can't put this in place without taking into account the needs of their clients," Ms. Clarke said.

RECRUITING IN TECH

Myfanwy Edwards spends a lot of time at universities, encouraging women to study technology and engineering.

Ms. Edwards, a programmer and engineer who has worked at the Japanese technology company Fujitsu since the 1980s, has risen

MICHAEL HIRSHON

Myfanwy Edwards is sometimes challenged by male colleagues for pushing a feminist agenda. "I say no — it's all of our problem," she said.

through the ranks and now works with management to recruit and promote women.

When she was hired, most of her colleagues at Fujitsu's offices in Britain were men. So were most of the company's clients.

Like many big companies, Fujitsu found that its gender pay gap stemmed mainly from an underrepresentation of women in senior management roles and in more highly paid areas, especially technical and sales positions.

To rectify that imbalance — women in the British operations are paid a median of 82 pounds for every 100 pounds earned by male colleagues — it has sought to promote female engineers and the work they do.

After rotating through different departments, Ms. Edwards was in 2014 the first woman to be named a "senior distinguished engineer," a companywide award. Today, 16 women have received those accolades. She was later elevated to an exclusive 10-person group of fellows that decides who will receive the distinguished engineer awards — but she is the only woman.

One of the biggest challenges is figuring out ways to increase the gender parity in the pipeline: only 16 percent of Britain's graduates in science, technology, engineering and math last year were women. Fujitsu is aiming to have women make up 20 percent of its engineers, 30 percent of its sales force and a quarter of its senior managers by 2020.

To get there, the company is focusing on recruiting. Ms. Edwards visits universities to encourage women to get into technology and engineering. Last year, at least half of all new apprentices were women, up from one-third in 2014.

Occasionally, a male colleague will challenge Ms. Edwards for pressing a feminist agenda.

"I say no — it's all of our problem," she said. The more gender equality conversations occur in the workplace, she added, the more men recognize the issue and are willing to support it.

Hannah Butson received training from her employer, Britain's biggest wine retailer, in wine tasting and blind taste tests. Afterwards, "it was really easy to describe a wine," she said.

"There is a problem that is being talked about, and men are going, 'Oh, yeah, I didn't think of that.'"

WOMEN IN WINE

Majestic Wine is a rare company in Britain — its gender pay data revealed that it pays women more than men.

That was mainly because most male employees work in lower-paid warehouse jobs, stacking wine pallets or lifting heavy loads.

Still, Majestic says it is eager to get even more women out front at its stores.

The only thing that Hannah Butson knew about reds, whites and rosés when she applied for a job at Britain's biggest wine retailer was that she liked to drink them.

But when Majestic Wine ushered her into training for a professional wine qualification, her ambitions grew. After intensive courses in wine tasting and blind taste tests, "it was really easy to describe a wine," she said. She was soon a senior assistant manager, and she now helps run a large store near London's financial district.

In a traditionally male-dominated industry, she remains one of the few women helping customers at the company's 210 British outlets. Two-thirds of Majestic's 1,500 employees are men, and only about a quarter of applicants for jobs are women.

"There is that real conception of an old man, swirling a glass, explaining all these flavors that they're getting from a wine," Ms. Butson said.

By having employees like Ms. Butson running tastings and finding wines for customers, Majestic is hoping it can throw off gender-related preconceptions about wine — and become a more attractive employer for women.

It is hard to get female recruits in the door, said Sarah Appleton, the company's head of human resources.

To attract more women, Majestic adjusted its job postings by dropping requirements for previous industry experience, to avoid evoking an image of wine as mainly a man's domain. (Recruiting language that seems masculine or feminine can create barriers and discourage women from applying, studies show.) It focused only on necessary skills and emphasized that wine knowledge could be taught within the company.

"If we require wine industry experience, the wine industry is male-dominated, so we're fishing in a pool of men," Ms. Appleton said.

Ms. Butson has seen changes already. She is working in a store with women for the first time since she started in 2016. Two of her three female colleagues applied for jobs after attending wine tastings.

"It's just about getting rid of that stigma that it is a male-dominated industry," Ms. Butson said.

AMIE TSANG reported from London and LIZ ALDERMAN from Paris.

Major Fashion Names Among Worst Offenders in Britain Gender Pay Gap

BY ELIZABETH PATON | APRIL 5, 2018

LONDON — This week, as the final hours ticked down to the deadline for British companies to report their gender pay gap data or face a fine, a flurry of last-minute filings revealed a stark and unflattering trend: Fashion and beauty brands, predominantly focused on female consumers and audiences, and often employing an overwhelmingly female staff, are among the worst offenders in the country when it comes to paying men more than women.

The explanation, according to several companies? A coterie of men in a handful of top-tier executive roles, while the majority of entry-level, retail, design and distribution center jobs are held by women, creating a gendered, pyramid employment structure reflected across sectors in the fashion industry.

Take Condé Nast Publications Limited, publisher of magazines such as Vogue, Vanity Fair, Glamour and GQ. The company reported data on Tuesday that revealed it to have the largest mean gender pay gap favoring men among all British media publishers and broadcasters, despite having more women than men at every pay quartile.

The company reported a mean gender pay gap of 36.9 percent (in other words, when comparing mean hourly rates, women earn 63 pence, or 83 cents, for every 1 pound, or $1.40, that men earn) and a median gap of 23 percent (when comparing median hourly rates, women earn 77 pence, or $1.08, for every £1, or $1.40, that men earn).

In a statement published alongside the data, Condé Nast attributed its salary skew to its longstanding and male-dominated senior leadership team. The chairman of Condé Nast Britain, Nicholas Coleridge, for example, has held various roles across the executive team since 1991. Jonathan Newhouse has led Condé Nast International for over 30 years. The statement said that across three-quarters of its business, the company had not found evidence of an appreciable gender pay gap. Three-quarters of all Condé Nast employees are female, with the bottom two salary quartiles particularly dominated by women.

The disparity of wages that exist within most fashion businesses was further underscored by the figures produced by many brands and retailers. The middle market women's wear brand Karen Millen pays women 49 percent less than men on a median hourly basis, meaning that, companywide, men's median pay was double that of women. Women made up 84 percent of the company's top positions, with a female C.E.O. and C.F.O., and the same proportion of men and women received bonuses, yet women's median bonus pay was 96 percent lower than men's.

In a statement, the company said that this was because the majority of its retail assistants and distribution center staff were women, and that the small percentage of male employees worked mostly in its head office.

"Our gender gap paints a misleading picture about our commitment to gender diversity and equality," the statement read, adding that when head office roles were excluded, the gender pay gap dropped to 6 percent. It did not, however, address why so many head office roles were filled by men instead of women.

Other high-profile names included Victoria's Secret, with a median hourly rate gap of 19 percent, and Benefit Cosmetics, which revealed a 30.7 percent median hourly rate gap, although women made up more than 90 percent of each pay quartile at the company. At Burberry, where women make up 70 percent of the luxury fashion group's employees, there is a 26 percent gender pay gap in favor of men, who get higher bonuses too. None of the companies in this article wished to provide further comment beyond the statements released with their data.

"While we continue to take steps to ensure employees at all levels are able to fulfill their potential and further their careers at Burberry, and are recognized for their contribution, we know we can do more," said the Burberry chief executive, Marco Gobbetti, when the company released its data last month. "This report shows that we have a gender pay gap in the U.K. The gap is influenced by the fact that we have fewer women in senior positions, however we are committed to narrowing this gap as we work to develop more women leaders to drive the growth and success of our business."

More than 2,500 companies, equivalent to one in four, submitted their gender pay gap figures in the 48 hours before midnight on Wednesday. Last year, the government ordered all British companies with more than 250 employees to publish their gender pay gap reports by midnight on April 4.

The hope, it said, was to shame companies into doing more to close the divide. On the final day of results, findings indicated that 78 percent of companies showed a pay gap in favor of men, 14 percent had a gap favoring women and 8 percent had no gender pay gap. The government calculated that Britain's overall pay gap is 18.1 percent.

Prime Minister Theresa May called the gender pay gap a "burning injustice," and added that the whole of society would remain "poorer" if outdated employment practices went unchallenged.

The effort in Britain is one of a growing number of initiatives among countries to promote equal pay. Australia recently mandated gender pay gap reporting for most companies, while in Germany a new law will require businesses with more than 500 employees to reveal their pay gaps. The fashion industry, riding high on selling female empowerment via T-shirt slogans and social media hashtags, is starting to look like the employer equivalent of the emperor's new clothes.

Glossary

anchoring bias A type of bias that relies disproportionately on an initial piece of information (known as the "anchor") in decision-making.

civil rights The rights of citizens to equal treatment, freedom and opportunities, regardless of race, sex or religion.

discrimination The unjust or prejudicial treatment of different types of people on the grounds of race, age or gender.

Equal Pay Act A law signed by John F. Kennedy in 1963 designed to abolish the gender pay gap.

Equal Pay Day The day each year, selected by the National Committee on Pay Equity, that women would have to work to in order to catch up with what their male counterparts earned the previous year.

"equal pay for equal work" A concept in labor rights that individuals in the same workplace performing equal work should receive equal pay.

gender pay gap The difference between the amounts paid to women and men, often calculated as an average across an organization or an economy.

incentive A payment, concession or other motivation that encourages an individual or an organization to do something.

litigation The process of taking legal action.

motherhood penalty A term coined by sociologists who suggest that women with children encounter systematic disadvantages in the workplace in terms of pay and benefits, compared to childless women.

parental leave An employee benefit that provides new parents time away from work without a change to their employment.

parity Equality, particularly in terms of status or pay.

Paycheck Fairness Act A proposed labor law that would strengthen protections to the Equal Pay Act. As of 2018, it has been introduced more than ten times, but yet to be passed by Congress.

pay transparency The process by which compensation levels are made public and employees are able to discuss and compare wages and salaries without recourse.

regulation A rule made by an authority that controls conduct.

restitution The restoration of something lost or stolen to its rightful owner; compensation for a certain loss.

salary history ban A law passed by some states and designed to combat the gender pay gap that prevents employers from asking a potential employee's past salary before hiring.

stagnation A lack of activity, growth, or development.

Title IX A federal civil rights law that forbids discrimination based on sex or gender.

Media Literacy Terms

"Media literacy" refers to the ability to access, understand, critically assess and create media. The following terms are important components of media literacy, and they will help you critically engage with the articles in this title.

angle The aspect of a news story that a journalist focuses on and develops.

attribution The method by which a source is identified or by which facts and information are assigned to the person who provided them.

balance Principle of journalism that both perspectives of an argument should be presented in a fair way.

bias A disposition of prejudice in favor of a certain idea, person or perspective.

column A type of story that is a regular feature, often on a recurring topic, written by the same journalist, generally known as a columnist.

commentary A type of story that is an expression of opinion on recent events by a journalist, generally known as a commentator.

credibility The quality of being trustworthy and believable, said of a journalistic source.

editorial Article of opinion or interpretation.

fake news A fictional or made-up story presented in the style of a legitimate news story, intended to deceive readers; also commonly used to criticize legitimate news because of its perspective or unfavorable coverage of a subject.

impartiality Principle of journalism that a story should not reflect a journalist's bias and should contain balance.

intention The motive or reason behind something, such as the publication of a news story.

motive The reason behind something, such as the publication of a news story or a source's perspective on an issue.

news story An article or style of expository writing that reports news, generally in a straightforward fashion and without editorial comment.

op-ed An opinion piece that reflects a prominent individual's opinion on a topic of interest.

paraphrase The summary of an individual's words, with attribution, rather than a direct quotation of the individual's exact words.

plagiarism An attempt to pass another person's work as one's own without attribution.

quotation The use of an individual's exact words indicated by the use of quotation marks and proper attribution.

reliability The quality of being dependable and accurate, said of a journalistic source.

source The origin of the information reported in journalism.

style A distinctive use of language in writing or speech; also a news or publishing organization's rules for consistent use of language with regards to spelling, punctuation, typography and capitalization, usually regimented by a house style guide.

tone A manner of expression in writing or speech.

Media Literacy Questions

1. Identify the various sources cited in the article "Dr. Paid Less: An Old Title Still Fits Female Physicians" (on page 47). How does Catherine Saint Louis attribute information to each of these sources in her article? How effective are her attributions in helping the reader identify her sources?

2. In "How to Close a Gender Gap: Let Employees Control Their Schedules" (on page 149), Claire Cain Miller paraphrases information from Erin Fahs. What are the strengths of the use of a paraphrase as opposed to a direct quote? What are the weaknesses?

3. Compare the headlines of "What We Talk About When We Talk About Pay Inequity" (on page 109) and "How to Attack the Gender Wage Gap? Speak Up" (on page 126). Which is a more compelling headline, and why? How could the less compelling headline be changed to better draw the reader's interest?

4. Do Michael D. Shear and Annie Lowrey demonstrate the journalistic principle of balance in their article "As Obama Spotlights Gender Gap in Wages, His Own Payroll Draws Scrutiny" (on page 73)? If so, how did they do so? If not, what could they have included to make their article more balanced?

5. The article "Carli Lloyd: Why I'm Fighting for Equal Pay" (on page 64) is an example of an op-ed. Identify how Carli Lloyd's attitude and tone help convey her opinion on the topic.

6. Does "Equal Pay for Men and Women? Iceland Wants Employers to Prove It" (on page 173) use multiple sources? What are the strengths of using multiple sources in a journalistic piece? What are the weaknesses of relying heavily on only one or a few sources?

7. What is the intention of the article "Let's Expose the Gender Pay Gap" (on page 132)? How effectively does it achieve its intended purpose?

8. Analyze the authors' perspective in "Gender Pay Gap? Maybe Not in the Corner Office, a Study Shows" (on page 76) and "Is Planned Parenthood's President Overpaid?" (on page 98). Do you think one journalist's reporting is more impartial than the other? If so, why do you think so?

9. Often, as a news story develops, a journalist's attitude toward a subject may change. Compare "The Motherhood Penalty vs. the Fatherhood Bonus" (on page 83) and "One Effort to Close the Gender Pay Gap Won't Get a Try Under Trump" (on page 153), both by Claire Cain Miller. Did new information discovered between the publication of these two articles change Claire Cain Miller's perspective?

10. Identify each of the sources in "How Boston Is Trying to Close the Gender Pay Gap" (on page 160) as a primary source or a secondary source. Evaluate the reliability and credibility of each source. How does your evaluation of each source change your perspective on this article?

Citations

All citations in this list are formatted according to the Modern Language Association's (MLA) style guide.

BOOK CITATION

NEW YORK TIMES EDITORIAL STAFF, THE. *The Gender Pay Gap: Equal Work, Unequal Pay.* New York: New York Times Educational Publishing, 2019.

ONLINE ARTICLE CITATIONS

ALDERMAN, LIZ. "Britain Aims to Close Gender Pay Gap With Transparency and Shame." *The New York Times*, 4 Apr. 2018, www.nytimes.com/2018/04/04/business/britain-gender-pay-gap.html.

ALDERMAN, LIZ. "Equal Pay for Men and Women? Iceland Wants Employers to Prove It." *The New York Times*, 28 Mar. 2017, www.nytimes.com/2017/03/28/business/economy/iceland-women-equal-pay.html.

ASTOR, MAGGIE. "Catt Sadler Leaves E! Entertainment, Saying a Male Co-Host Earned Twice as Much." *The New York Times*, 20 Dec. 2017, www.nytimes.com/2017/12/20/arts/television/catt-sadler-e-equal-pay.html.

BENNETT, JESSICA. "How to Attack the Gender Wage Gap? Speak Up." *The New York Times*, 15 Dec. 2012, https://www.nytimes.com/2012/12/16/business/to-solve-the-gender-wage-gap-learn-to-speak-up.html.

BERNARD, TARA SIEGEL. "Another Reason Women May Be Paid Less Than Men." *The New York Times*, 30 July 2012, bucks.blogs.nytimes.com/2012/07/30/another-reason-why-women-may-be-paid-less-than-men.

BERNARD, TARA SIEGEL. "Vigilant Eye on Gender Pay Gap." *The New York Times*, 14 Nov. 2014, www.nytimes.com/2014/11/15/business/keeping-a-vigilant-eye-on-pay-equity-for-women.html.

BLOW, CHARLES M. " 'Williams,' the Princess and the Gender Pay Gap." *The New York Times*, 5 Feb. 2014, www.nytimes.com/2014/02/06/opinion/blow-williams-the-princess-and-the-gender-pay-gap.html.

CHAN, SEWELL. "BBC Publishes Pay of Top Stars, Revealing Gender Gap." *The New York Times*, 19 July 2017, www.nytimes.com/2017/07/19/world/europe /bbc-salaries-pay-gender.html.

COWLEY, STACY. "Illegal in Massachusetts: Asking Your Salary in a Job Interview." *The New York Times*, 2 Aug. 2016, www.nytimes.com/2016/08/03 /business/dealbook/wage-gap-massachusetts-law-salary-history.html.

DAS, ANDREW. "Top Female Players Accuse U.S. Soccer of Wage Discrimination." *The New York Times*, 31 Mar. 2016, www.nytimes.com/2016/04/01 /sports/soccer/uswnt-us-women-carli-lloyd-alex-morgan-hope-solo -complain.html.

DAVIS, JULIE HIRSCHFELD. "Obama Moves to Expand Rules Aimed at Closing Gender Pay Gap." *The New York Times*, 29 Jan. 2016, www.nytimes.com /2016/01/29/us/politics/obama-moves-to-expand-rules-aimed-at-closing -gender-pay-gap.html.

GOLDIN, CLAUDIA. "How to Win the Battle of the Sexes Over Pay (Hint: It Isn't Simple.)." *The New York Times*, 10 Nov. 2017, www.nytimes .com/2017/11/10/business/how-to-win-the-battle-of-the-sexes-over -pay-.html.

GREENHOUSE, LINDA. "Justices' Ruling Limits Suits on Pay Disparity." *The New York Times*, 30 May 2007, www.nytimes.com/2007/05/30/washington /30scotus.html.

HAAG, MATTHEW. "BBC News Editor Quits Her Post to Protest Gender Pay Gap." *The New York Times*, 7 Jan. 2018, www.nytimes.com/2018/01/07 /business/media/bbc-gender-pay-gap.html.

HAIGNEY, SOPHIE. "Emma Stone Says Male Co-Stars Cut Their Own Salaries to Tackle Inequity." *The New York Times*, 7 July 2017, www.nytimes.com /2017/07/07/movies/emma-stone-male-costars-salaries.html.

LEONHARDT, DAVID. "Gender Pay Gap, Once Narrowing, Is Stuck in Place." *The New York Times*, 24 Dec. 2006, https://www.nytimes.com/2006/12/24 /business/24gap.html.

LIPMAN, JOANNE. "Let's Expose the Gender Pay Gap." *The New York Times*, 13 Aug. 2015, www.nytimes.com/2015/08/13/opinion/lets-expose-the -gender-pay-gap.html.

LLOYD, CARLI. "Carli Lloyd: Why I'm Fighting for Equal Pay." *The New York Times*, 10 Apr. 2016, www.nytimes.com/2016/04/11/sports/soccer/carli-lloyd -why-im-fighting-for-equal-pay.html.

MAYS, JEFFERY C. "Mark Wahlberg and Agency Will Donate $2 Million to

Time's Up After Outcry Over Pay." *The New York Times*, 13 Jan. 2018, www
.nytimes.com/2018/01/13/arts/mark-wahlberg-michelle-williams.html.

MILLER, CLAIRE CAIN. "Children Hurt Women's Earnings, but Not Men's (Even in
Scandinavia)." *The New York Times*, 5 Feb. 2018, www.nytimes.com/2018/02
/05/upshot/even-in-family-friendly-scandinavia-mothers-are-paid-less.html.

MILLER, CLAIRE CAIN. "The Gender Pay Gap Is Largely Because of Motherhood." *The New York Times*, 13 May 2017, www.nytimes.com/2017/05/13
/upshot/the-gender-pay-gap-is-largely-because-of-motherhood.html.

MILLER, CLAIRE CAIN. "How a Common Interview Question Fuels the Gender
Pay Gap (and How to Stop It)." *The New York Times*, 1 May 2018, www
.nytimes.com/2018/05/01/upshot/how-a-common-interview-question
-fuels-the-gender-pay-gap-and-how-to-stop-it.html.

MILLER, CLAIRE CAIN. "How to Bridge That Stubborn Pay Gap." *The New York
Times*, 15 Jan. 2016, www.nytimes.com/2016/01/17/upshot/how-to-bridge
-that-stubborn-pay-gap.html.

MILLER, CLAIRE CAIN. "How to Close a Gender Gap: Let Employees Control
Their Schedules." *The New York Times*, 7 Feb. 2017, www.nytimes.com/2017
/02/07/upshot/how-to-close-a-gender-gap-let-employees-control-their
-schedules.html.

MILLER, CLAIRE CAIN. "The Motherhood Penalty vs. the Fatherhood Bonus."
The New York Times, 6 Sept. 2014, www.nytimes.com/2014/09/07/upshot
/a-child-helps-your-career-if-youre-a-man.html.

MILLER, CLAIRE CAIN. "One Effort to Close the Gender Pay Gap Won't Get a
Try Under Trump." *The New York Times*, 31 Aug. 2017, www.nytimes.com
/2017/08/31/upshot/one-effort-to-close-the-gender-pay-gap-wont-get-a
-try.html.

MILLER, CLAIRE CAIN. "The 10-Year Baby Window That Is the Key to the
Women's Pay Gap." *The New York Times*, 9 Apr. 2018, www.nytimes
.com/2018/04/09/upshot/the-10-year-baby-window-that-is-the-key-to
-the-womens-pay-gap.html.

MILLER, CLAIRE CAIN. "As Women Take Over a Male-Dominated Field, the Pay
Drops." *The New York Times*, 18 Mar. 2016, www.nytimes.com/2016
/03/20/upshot/as-women-take-over-a-male-dominated-field-the-pay
-drops.html.

MULLAINATHAN, SENDHIL. "Possible Path to Closing Pay Gap." *The New York
Times*, 10 May 2014, www.nytimes.com/2014/05/11/upshot/a-possible-path
-to-closing-the-pay-gap.html.

THE NEW YORK TIMES. "Room for Debate: How to Reduce the Pay Gap Between Men and Women." *The New York Times*, 15 Aug. 2016, www.nytimes.com/roomfordebate/2016/08/15/how-to-reduce-the-pay-gap-between-men-and-women.

THE NEW YORK TIMES. "Women Still Earn a Lot Less Than Men." *The New York Times*, 14 Apr. 2015, www.nytimes.com/2015/04/14/opinion/women-still-earn-a-lot-less-than-men.html.

OLSON, ELIZABETH. "A 44% Pay Divide for Female and Male Law Partners, Survey Says." *The New York Times*, 12 Oct. 2016, www.nytimes.com/2016/10/13/business/dealbook/female-law-partners-earn-44-less-than-the-men-survey-shows.html.

PATON, ELIZABETH. "Major Fashion Names Among Worst Offenders in Britain Gender Pay Gap." *The New York Times*, 5 Apr. 2018, www.nytimes.com/2018/04/05/fashion/uk-fashion-companies-gender-pay-gap.html.

PEAR, ROBERT. "Courts Cases Reveal New Inequalities in Women's Pay." *The New York Times*, 21 Aug. 1985, https://www.nytimes.com/1985/08/21/garden/court-cases-reveal-new-inequalities-in-women-s-pay.html.

PLASS, SARAH. "Wage Gaps for Women Frustrating Germany." *The New York Times*, 2 Sept. 2008, www.nytimes.com/2008/09/03/business/worldbusiness/03women.html.

ROTHENBERG, BEN. "Roger Federer, $731,000; Serena Williams, $495,000: The Pay Gap in Tennis." *The New York Times*, 12 Apr. 2016, www.nytimes.com/2016/04/13/sports/tennis/equal-pay-gender-gap-grand-slam-majors-wta-atp.html.

SAFRONOVA, VALERIYA. "What We Talk About When We Talk About Pay Inequity." *The New York Times*, 3 Feb. 2018, www.nytimes.com/2018/02/03/business/wage-gap-gender-discrimination.html.

SAINT LOUIS, CATHERINE. "Dr. Paid Less: An Old Title Still Fits Female Physicians." *The New York Times*, 11 July 2016, www.nytimes.com/2016/07/12/health/women-doctors-salaries-pay-gap.html.

SAINT LOUIS, CATHERINE. "Stubborn Pay Gap Is Found in Nursing." *The New York Times*, 24 Mar. 2015, https://well.blogs.nytimes.com/2015/03/24/stubborn-pay-gap-is-found-in-nursing/.

SANGER-KATZ, MARGOT, AND CLAIRE CAIN MILLER. "Is Planned Parenthood's President Overpaid?" *The New York Times*, 30 Sept. 2015, www.nytimes.com/2015/10/01/upshot/is-planned-parenthoods-president-overpaid.html.

SHEAR, MICHAEL D., AND ANNIE LOWREY. "As Obama Spotlights Gender Gap in Wages, His Own Payroll Draws Scrutiny." *The New York Times*, 7 Apr. 2014,

www.nytimes.com/2014/04/08/us/politics/as-obama-spotlights-gender-gap
-in-wages-his-own-payroll-draws-scrutiny.html.

SHEETS, HILARIE M. "Study Finds a Gender Gap at the Top Museums." *The New York Times*, 7 Mar. 2014, www.nytimes.com/2014/03/08/arts/design /study-finds-a-gender-gap-at-the-top-museums.html.

SORKIN, ANDREW ROSS. "Gender Pay Gap? Maybe Not in the Corner Office, a Study Shows." *The New York Times*, 23 Apr. 2018, www.nytimes.com/2018 /04/23/business/dealbook/ceo-gender-pay-gap.html.

STETSON, DAMON. "Law in Effect Today Bans Job Discrimination Based on Sex." *The New York Times*, 10 June 1964, https://www.nytimes.com/1964 /06/10/archives/law-in-effect-today-bans-job-discrimination-based-on -sex.html.

STOLBERG, SHERYL GAY. "Obama Signs Equal-Pay Legislation." *The New York Times*, 29 Jan. 2009, www.nytimes.com/2009/01/30/us/politics/30ledbetter -web.html.

SUSSMAN, ANNA LOUIE. "How Boston Is Trying to Close the Gender Pay Gap." *The New York Times*, 26 May 2018, www.nytimes.com/2018/05/26/business /gender-pay-gap-boston.html.

TSANG, AMIE. "British Companies Must Reveal How They Pay Women vs. Men." *The New York Times*, 6 Apr. 2017, www.nytimes.com/2017/04/06 /business/britain-salary-gender-gap.html.

TSANG, AMIE, AND LIZ ALDERMAN. "The Gender Pay Gap: Trying to Narrow It." *The New York Times*, 13 May 2018, www.nytimes.com/2018/05/13/business /gender-pay-britain.html.

WAKABAYASHI, DAISUKE. "At Google, Employee-Led Effort Finds Men Are Paid More Than Women." *The New York Times*, 8 Sept. 2017, www.nytimes.com /2017/09/08/technology/google-salaries-gender-disparity.html.

WILLIAMS, JACQUELINE. "Australian TV Host's Departure Raises Questions on Gender Pay Gap." *The New York Times*, 17 Oct. 2017, www.nytimes.com/2017 /10/17/world/australia/gender-pay-gap-lisa-wilkinson.html.

Index

This book is current up until the time of printing. For the most up-to-date reporting, visit www.nytimes.com.